Designing Tasks for the Communicative Classroom

CAMBRIDGE LANGUAGE TEACHING LIBRARY
A series of authoritative books on subjects of central importance for all
language teachers.

In this series:

Designing Tasks for the Communicative Classroom

David Nunan

National Centre for English Language Teaching and Research,
Macquarie University, Sydney

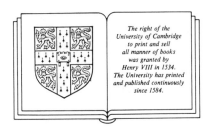

The right of the
University of Cambridge
to print and sell
all manner of books
was granted by
Henry VIII in 1534.
The University has printed
and published continuously
since 1584.

Cambridge University Press
Cambridge
New York   Port Chester
Melbourne   Sydney

Published by the Press Syndicate of the University of Cambridge
The Pitt Building, Trumpington Street, Cambridge CB2 1RP
40 West 20th Street, New York, NY 10011, USA
10 Stamford Road, Oakleigh, Melbourne 3166, Australia

© Cambridge University Press 1989

First published 1989
Third printing 1990

Printed in Great Britain by Bell & Bain Ltd, Glasgow

Library of Congress cataloguing in publication data

Nunan, David.
Designing tasks for the communicative classroom / David Nunan.
    p.   cm. – (Cambridge language teaching library).
Includes bibliographies and index.
1. Language and languages – Study and teaching.
2. Communicative competence. I. Title.   II. Series.
P53.N86 1989
418'.007–dc19   88–31883 CIP

British Library cataloguing in publication data

Nunan, David
Designing tasks for the communicative classroom –
(Cambridge language teaching library).
1. Foreign languages. Teaching.
I. Title.
418'.007

ISBN 0 521 37014 0 hardback
ISBN 0 521 37915 6 paperback

CE

Dedication

To Jennifer and Rebecca
for the unread stories and the unplayed games

Contents

Contents

Acknowledgements

I should like to thank Adrian du Plessis and Annemarie Young from Cambridge University Press who encouraged me to undertake the writing of this book, and whose advice along the way was invaluable.

I should also like to thank Jane Lockwood and Jack Richards for their advice and support.

Most of all I owe an enormous debt of gratitude to Roger Bowers whose detailed criticism of earlier drafts had a major impact on the final shape of the book. Needless to say, any shortcomings in the book are mine alone.

The author and publishers would like to thank the following for permission to reproduce copyright material:

Addison-Wesley Publishing Company (Sydney) for A. Morris and N. Stewart-Dore (1984) *Learning to learn from text: effective reading in the content areas* pp. 46, 50, 101–2; Adelaide College of Technical and Further Education for H. Forrester, L. Palmer and P. Spinks (1986) *It's over to you* p. 18; Cambridge University Press for A. Doff, C. Jones and K. Mitchell (1983) *Meaning into words: Intermediate* p. 57; F. Grellet (1981) *Developing reading skills* pp. 12–13; L. Hamp-Lyons and B. Heasley (1987) *Study writing* pp. 8–9; D. Hover (1986) *Think twice* pp. 45–8; L. Jones (1985) *Use of English* pp. 36–7 A. Maley and S. Moulding (1981) *Learning to listen* pp. 3–5; D. Nunan and J. Lockwood (1988) *The Australian English course:* Level 1, draft pilot edition; P. Pattison (1987) *Developing communication skills* pp. 7–8; G. Wells (1981) *Learning through interaction* pp. 24–5; Language Press, Adelaide for D. Nunan (1982) *What do you think?*; Longman Ltd. for B. Abbs, C. Candlin, C. Edelhoff, T. Moston and M. Sexton (1978) *Challenges* Students' Book pp. 2–14; C. Candlin and C. Edelhoff (1982) *Challenges* Teacher's Book p. 26; Ministry of Education, Melbourne for R. Evans (1986) *Learning English through content areas: the topic approach to ESL* p. 7; Ministry of Education and Youth, Sultanate of Oman for D. Nunan (1989) *Syllabus specifications for the Omani school English language curriculum*; National Curriculum Resource Centre, Adelaide for J. Clemens and J. Crawford (1986) *Lifelines* p. 133; M. Jones and R. Moar (1985) *Listen to Australia* Teacher's Book p. 126, Students' Book pp. 97, 99, 101; D. Slade and L. Norris (1986) *Teaching casual conversation* p. 81; Oxford University Press for D. Nunan (1988) *Syllabus design* pp. 56–7; N. Prabhu (1987) *Second language pedagogy: a perspective* pp. 46–7; T. Wright (1987) *Roles of teachers and learners* p. 58; Oxford University Press

Acknowledgements

A Practical Guide to the Teaching of English as a Second or Foreign Language by Wilga M. Rivers and Mary S. Temperley p. 4. Copyright © Oxford University Press. Reprinted by permission. TESOL for *'Information gap' tasks: Do they facilitate second language acquisition?* by C. Doughty and T. Pica, 1986. TESOL Quarterly 20 (2) pp. 305–25. Copyright by TESOL 1986. Reprinted by permission.

Introduction

The purpose of the book

The purpose of this book is to provide teachers with a practical introduction to the design and development of communicative language learning tasks. Although the idea of using the learning 'task' as a basic planning tool is not a new one in the general educational field, it is a relatively recent arrival on the language teaching scene, and there remains some confusion about the place of tasks within the curriculum. The central question here is: should the specification of learning tasks be seen as part of syllabus design or of methodology?

In this book, I shall argue that, with the development of communicative language teaching, the separation of syllabus design and methodology becomes increasingly problematical. If we maintain the traditional distinction between syllabus design and methodology, seeing syllabus design as being primarily concerned with the specification of what learners will learn, and methodology as being mainly concerned with specifying how learners will learn, then the design of learning tasks is part of methodology. However, if we see curriculum planning as an integrated set of processes involving, among other things, the specification of both what and how, then the argument over whether the design and development of tasks belongs to syllabus design or to methodology becomes unimportant.

The examples of learning tasks in the book have been taken from a variety of sources. The ideas presented are relevant to teachers working in, or preparing for, a range of situations with a variety of learner types. Thus, it should be useful to teachers of children as well as of adults, to foreign as well as second language teachers, and to teachers of ESP (English for Specific Purposes) as well as of general purpose English.

Alongside the practical aspects of the subject, I have tried to deal with theoretical issues in ways which are non-trivial, yet are accessible to non-specialists.

It tends to be the custom, in books of this sort, to append a list of questions to the end of each chapter. I have adopted a rather different approach by inserting questions into the text itself. At various points readers will find that they are invited to reflect on key points and questions, and relate these to their own situation. While the answers I would give to some of the questions will emerge in the subsequent text, for other questions there are no easy answers, or there may be no widespread consensus on what might count as an appropriate answer.

For much of this century, language teaching has been preoccupied with methods. In some extreme cases this has led to a search for the 'right method'. Methods tend to exist as package deals, each with its own set of principles and operating procedures, each with its own set of preferred learning tasks.

In this book, I shall have very little to say about 'methods'. I do not accept that there is such a thing as the 'right method', and I do not intend to assign different tasks to different methodological pigeon-holes. Rather, I shall look at tasks in terms of their goals, the input data, linguistic or otherwise, on which they are based, the activities derived from the input, and the roles and settings implied by different tasks for teachers and learners. I shall also look at the issues involved in sequencing and integrating tasks, as well as at the factors to be considered in grading tasks. The final chapter of the book is devoted to an exploration of the role of tasks in teacher development, particularly in the use of task analysis as a means of encouraging a reflective methodology; that is, planning one's teaching on the basis of what actually happens in classrooms rather than on abstract statements about what should happen.

Traditional approaches to methodology tend to analyse tasks in terms of the macroskills of listening, speaking, reading and writing. While most tasks take one or other of the macroskills as their principal point of focus, I have chosen to organise this analysis around what I consider to be three central characteristics: task goals, input, and activities. We shall also look at settings and learner and teacher roles implied by tasks. There are several reasons for adopting this approach rather than analysing tasks purely in terms of macroskills. In the first place, few tasks involve only one skill. It is rare that one only reads, or listens, or speaks, or writes. Therefore, it is often difficult to assign tasks to one skill label or another. Secondly, I hope to encourage teachers to think more about the integration and sequencing of tasks. The major purpose of this book then is to provide teachers with a framework for analysing learning tasks which will help them select, adapt or create their own learning tasks. I hope that the book might be of some assistance in assigning the search for the one right method to the dustbin and in helping teachers develop, select or adapt tasks which are appropriate in terms of goals, input, activities, roles and settings, and difficulty.

The structure of the book

Chapter 1 sets out some of the basic issues in relation to communicative learning tasks. The sense in which the term 'task' is to be used in the rest of the book is established, and the place of tasks within the curriculum is outlined. There is a short section on communicative language teaching, and the role of the learner is discussed.

Chapter 2 considers some of the central issues involved in language and learning relating these to tasks. We shall look in particular at what is involved in listening, speaking, reading and writing in another language. The debate over whether tasks should have a real-world or pedagogic rationale is presented and we shall look at how tasks are related to the wider curriculum through the specification of goals.

In Chapter 3 we look at the central characteristics of tasks and a scheme is presented for analysing tasks. I suggest that, minimally, communicative tasks consist of some form of input data plus an activity. The input may be linguistic (i.e. spoken or written language) non-linguistic (picture, sequences, diagrams, photos etc.) or a combination of the two (charts, maps, illustrated instructions etc.). These form the point of departure for the task. The activity specifies what learners are to do with the input. We shall examine some of the central issues surrounding the selection of data and activities, looking in particular at the issues of authenticity and activity focus.

Chapter 4 looks at the roles for teachers and learners which are implicit in any task. We shall see how these roles change as the focus of the activity changes, and we shall explore some of the classroom implications of role variability.

In Chapters 5 and 6, there is a shift of attention. We are no longer concerned with the characteristics of tasks in isolation, but with tasks in relation to one another. Chapter 5 is concerned with some of the issues and difficulties involved in grading tasks. Chapter 6 presents the options available in sequencing and integrating tasks to form lessons or units of work.

Chapter 7 is devoted to tasks and teacher development. We take further the notion, introduced in Chapter 1, that tasks form a useful point of entry into the study of the curriculum. We look at task construction and evaluation, and suggestions are made for introducing tasks in teacher development workshops.

1 Learning tasks and the language curriculum

1.1 Introduction

This chapter introduces the task as a basic building block in the language curriculum. We shall look at some definitions of the term, and see how tasks are related to other elements in the curriculum.

1.2 'Task' defined and described

What is a task?

In turning to the concept of 'task', the first thing we need to do is decide just what we mean by the term itself.

   If we look at what other people have written, we find that the term has been defined in a variety of ways. In general education, and in other fields such as psychology, there are many different definitions of tasks. There is also quite a variety from within the field of second language teaching, as the following definitions show.

> [a task is] a piece of work undertaken for oneself or for others, freely or for some reward. Thus, examples of tasks include painting a fence, dressing a child, filling out a form, buying a pair of shoes, making an airline reservation, borrowing a library book, taking a driving test, typing a letter, weighing a patient, sorting letters, taking a hotel reservation, writing a cheque, finding a street destination and helping someone across a road. In other words, by 'task' is meant the hundred and one things people do in everyday life, at work, at play, and in between.
>
> (Long 1985: 89)

This first definition is a non-technical, non-linguistic one. In fact, as the author points out, it describes the sorts of things that non-linguists would tell you they do if they were to be asked. (In the same way as learners, if asked why they are attending a language course, are more likely to say, 'So I can talk to my neighbours', than, 'So I can master the use of the subjunctive'.) The second thing to notice is that some of the examples provided may well not involve language (one can paint a fence without talking). Finally, the tasks may be subsidiary components of a larger task: for example, the task of 'weighing a patient' may be a sub-component of the task 'giving a medical examination'.

This final point in fact raises a major problem with the concept of 'task' as a unit of analysis. Where do we draw the boundaries? How do we decide where one task ends and the next begins?

> You might like to consider how many discrete tasks there are in the extract on pages 7–9. Is there a single task with separate phases, or several tasks? (I shall present my own view later in the chapter.)

Now here is another definition, this time from a dictionary of applied linguistics:

> an activity or action which is carried out as the result of processing or understanding language (i.e. as a response). For example, drawing a map while listening to a tape, listening to an instruction and performing a command, may be referred to as tasks. Tasks may or may not involve the production of language. A task usually requires the teacher to specify what will be regarded as successful completion of the task. The use of a variety of different kinds of tasks in language teaching is said to make language teaching more communicative . . . since it provides a purpose for a classroom activity which goes beyond the practice of language for its own sake.
>
> (Richards, Platt and Weber 1986: 289)

In this second definition, we see that the authors take a pedagogical perspective. Tasks are defined in terms of what the learner will do in the classroom rather than in the outside world. This distinction between what might be called 'pedagogic' tasks and 'real-world' tasks is an important one, and one which we shall look at in detail in Chapter 2.

The final definition is from Breen:

> . . . any structured language learning endeavour which has a particular objective, appropriate content, a specified working procedure, and a range of outcomes for those who undertake the task. 'Task' is therefore assumed to refer to a range of workplans which have the overall purpose of facilitating language learning – from the simple and brief exercise type, to more complex and lengthy activities such as group problem-solving or simulations and decision making.
>
> (Breen 1987: 23)

⟫→ *p. 10*

Pre-listening

1 a) Look carefully at this questionnaire.

What are your sleeping habits?

A short questionnaire
to discover your
sleeping habits

1 How much time do you
 spend on bedmaking?
 a) 5 mins a day
 b) 5 mins every other day
 c) 5 mins a week

2 Before you go to bed do you
 a) pull open the downstairs
  curtains
 b) read
 c) eat

3 After a night's sleep do you
 find that the covers
 a) are as tidy as when you went
  to bed
 b) are all over the floor
 c) are in a heap in the middle of
  the bed

4 If you have trouble getting to
 sleep do you
 a) count sheep
 b) toss and turn
 c) lie still and concentrate

5 If you wake up in the middle
 of the night is it because
 a) you remember something
  you ought to have done
 b) you're cold
 c) you're hungry

6 If you hear a bump in the
 night do you
 a) get up cautiously and
  investigate quietly
 b) charge around the house
  with a weapon
 c) turn over and go back to sleep

7 Do other people complain
 about your sleeping habits?
 a) never
 b) frequently
 c) sometimes

8 When you have dreams are
 they mostly
 a) dreams about work
 b) nightmares
 c) sweet dreams

Make sure that you understand all the words in it and that
you know how they are pronounced.

b) Now, working in pairs, one of you should interview the
other using this questionnaire. If there is time, change roles
(that is, the interviewer should now be interviewed).

Maley and Moulding: Learning to Listen, p. 3

Listening

2 a) You will now hear a recorded interview on the tape. You should work on your own. As you listen, note down which of the suggested answers is nearest to the one given on the tape. If none of them fit, then try to note down what the answer was. Do not worry if you do not get all the information the first time. You will hear the tape at least three times. ☞⚿

  b) When you have finished, work with a partner and compare your answers. Then check your answers with the teacher.

3 a) Stay with the same partner. You will now hear a second version of the interview. This time the interviewer does not ask all the questions and they are not in the same order as in the printed questionnaire. Once again try to decide which of the printed answers is nearest to the one given on the tape. ☞⚿

  b) When you have finished, compare your answers in groups of four. Then check them with the teacher.

Intensive listening

4 a) Listen carefully to the first interview again, in pairs. This time try to find which of the man's sentences match the following reported sentences.
  e.g. He explained that he had very little time.
  'Well I'm in a bit of a hurry.'

  i)   He expressed concern that the interviewer might be invading his privacy.
  ii) His opinion was that bedmaking was women's work.
  iii) He had been told that he did not move much in his sleep.
  iv) He answered that generally he had no problems in getting to sleep.
  v)   He disagreed that he was courageous – simply annoyed.
  vi) He denied that other people had complained.
  vii) He explained that he almost always forgot his dreams.
  Check your answers with those of another pair. ☞⚿

4 b) Now do the same thing using interview 2.
- i) He expressed reservations about the type of questions.
- ii) He explained that he rarely had any difficulty in falling asleep.
- iii) He explained that reading sent him to sleep.
- iv) He found his dreams somewhat disturbing.
- v) He denied that he snored.
- vi) He agreed that he occupied more than half of the bed.
- vii) He dismissed any complaints that people made. ⚷

Checking up

5 a) Listen to interview 1 again in groups of four. As you listen, note down in your own way (don't worry about the spelling) any words or phrases which you still do not understand. When you have finished, compare your notes with the others in the group. Perhaps someone else can help explain what you did not understand, and you may be able to help others. Finally, check any remaining problems by reading through the transcript on pages 51–5.

b) If there is time, work through interview 2 in the same way.

Maley and Moulding: Learning to Listen, pp. 4 and 5

> You might like to pause at this point and consider the similarities and differences between the three definitions which have been offered here. You might also like to think about which definition is most useful and meaningful for you.

The definitions we have looked at share one thing in common: they all imply that tasks involve communicative language use in which the user's attention is focused on meaning rather than linguistic structure. This is evident in the examples provided. Long mentions filling out a form, making an airline reservation, taking a driving test, etc. Richards *et al.* refer to drawing a map, listening to instructions and carrying out a command. Breen talks about problem solving and decision making (although his definition does allow for 'brief exercise types' which might conceivably include non-communicative tasks).

In general, I too will consider the communicative task as *a piece of classroom work which involves learners in comprehending, manipulating, producing or interacting in the target language while their attention is principally focused on meaning rather than form.* The task should also have a sense of completeness, being able to stand alone as a communicative act in its own right.

As we explore the development of tasks, we shall see that it is not always easy to draw a hard and fast distinction between 'communicative' and 'non-communicative' tasks. There are several reasons for this, not the least of which is the fact that meaning and form are closely interrelated. We use different grammatical forms to signal differences of meaning. In fact, good oral grammar exercises can and should be both meaningful and communicative.

What are the components of a task?

I shall want to suggest that, in analytic terms, tasks will contain some form of input data which might be verbal (for example a dialogue or reading passage) or non-verbal (for example a picture sequence) and an activity which is in some way derived from the input and which sets out what the learners are to do in relation to the input. The task will also have (implicitly or explicitly) a goal and roles for teachers and learners. In synthetic terms, we shall find, lessons and units of work will consist, among other things, of sequences of tasks, and the coherence of such lessons or units will depend on the extent to which the tasks have been integrated and sequenced in some principled way.

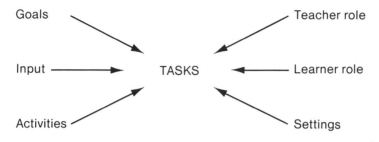

A framework for analysing communicative tasks

Let us consider your response to the extract from Maley and Moulding. There are five 'phases' to the unit. Some of these clearly qualify as communicative tasks, while others are less certain. The pre-listening, for example, is clearly a communicative task, as learners are involved in processing and producing language for communicative ends. The task is also complete in its own right. It can be characterised as follows:

Goal: Exchanging personal information
Input: Questionnaire on sleeping habits
Activity: i) Reading questionnaire
               ii) Asking and answering questions about sleeping habits
Teacher role: Monitor and facilitator
Learner role: Conversational partner
Setting: Classroom/pair work

Other phases in the unit are less clearly communicative, focusing learners on formal aspects of the language. However, it is important to bear in mind that it is not always easy to provide a simple definition or test which will give us a hard and fast method of distinguishing communicative tasks from other exercise and activity types, or of determining where one task ends and another begins. Making such decisions will always be partly intuitive and judgemental.

At this point, the description I have given may seem rather vague and imprecise. However, my characterisation of 'task' will become clearer once we have worked through a range of examples. For now, let us say that the task is a piece of meaning-focused work involving learners in comprehending, producing and/or interacting in the target language, and that tasks are analysed or categorised according to their goals, input data, activities, settings and roles.

1.3 Communicative language teaching

From the remarks already made, it should be obvious that the current interest in tasks stems largely from what has been termed 'the communicative approach' to language teaching. In this section I should like to briefly sketch out some of the more important principles underpinning communicative language teaching.

Although it is not always immediately apparent, everything we do in the classroom is underpinned by beliefs about the nature of language and about language learning. (We shall look at some of these beliefs in Chapter 2.) In recent years there have been some dramatic shifts in attitude towards both language and learning. This has sometimes resulted in contradictory messages to the teaching profession which, in turn, has led to confusion.

Among other things, it has been accepted that language is more than simply a system of rules. Language is now generally seen as a dynamic resource for the creation of meaning. In terms of learning, it is generally accepted that we need to distinguish between 'learning that' and 'knowing how'. In other words, we need to distinguish between knowing various grammatical rules and being able to use the rules effectively and appropriately when communicating.

This view has underpinned communicative language teaching (CLT). A great deal has been written and said about CLT, and it is something of a misnomer to talk about 'the communicative approach' as there is a family of approaches, each member of which claims to be 'communicative' (in fact, it is difficult to find approaches which claim not to be communicative!). There is also frequent disagreement between different members of the communicative family.

During the seventies, the insight that communication was an integrated process rather than a set of discrete learning outcomes created a dilemma for syllabus designers, whose task has traditionally been to produce ordered lists of structural, functional or notional items graded according to difficulty, frequency or pedagogic convenience. Processes belong to the domain of methodology. They are somebody else's business. They cannot be reduced to lists of items. For a time, it seems, the syllabus designer was to be out of business.

One of the clearest presentations of a syllabus proposal based on processes rather than products has come from Breen. He suggests that an alternative to the listing of linguistic content (the end point, as it were, in the learner's journey) would be to:

> . . . prioritize the route itself; a focusing upon the means towards the learning of a new language. Here the designer would give priority to the changing process of learning and the potential of the classroom – to the psychological and social resources applied to a

new language by learners in the classroom context. . . . a greater
concern with capacity for communication rather than repertoire of
communication, with the activity of learning a language viewed as
important as the language itself, and with a focus upon means
rather than predetermined objectives, all indicate priority of
process over content.

(Breen 1984: 52–3)

What Breen is suggesting is that, with communication at the centre of the
curriculum, the goal of that curriculum (individuals who are capable of
using the target language to communicate with others) and the means
(classroom activities which develop this capability) begin to merge; the
syllabus must take account of both the ends and the means.

What then do we do with our more formal approaches to the
specification of structures and skills? Can they be found a place in CLT?
We can focus on this issue by considering the place of grammar.

For some time after the rise of CLT, the status of grammar in the
curriculum was rather uncertain. Some linguists maintained that it was
not necessary to teach grammar, that the ability to use a second language
(knowing 'how') would develop automatically if the learner were
required to focus on meaning in the process of using the language to
communicate. In recent years, this view has come under serious chal-
lenge, and it now seems to be widely accepted that there is value in
classroom tasks which require learners to focus on form. It is also
accepted that grammar is an essential resource in using language communicatively.

This is certainly Littlewood's view. In his introduction to communicative language teaching, he suggests that the following skills need to be
taken into consideration:

- The learner must attain as high a degree as possible of linguistic
  competence. That is, he must develop skill in manipulating the
  linguistic system, to the point where he can use it spontaneously
  and flexibly in order to express his intended message.
- The learner must distinguish between the forms he has mastered
  as part of his linguistic competence, and the communicative
  functions which they perform. In other words, items mastered as
  part of a linguistic system must also be understood as part of a
  communicative system.
- The learner must develop skills and strategies for using language
  to communicate meanings as effectively as possible in concrete
  situations. He must learn to use feedback to judge his success,
  and if necessary, remedy failure by using different language.
- The learner must become aware of the social meaning of
  language forms. For many learners, this may not entail the
  ability to vary their own speech to suit different social

13

circumstances, but rather the ability to use generally acceptable
forms and avoid potentially offensive ones.

(Littlewood 1981: 6)

> At this point, you might like to consider your own
> position on this matter. Do you think that
> considerations of content selection and grading (i.e.
> selecting and grading grammar, functions, notions,
> topics, pronunciation, vocabulary etc.) should be kept
> separate from the selection and grading of tasks, or not?

As I have already pointed out, I take the view that any comprehensive
curriculum needs to take account of both means and ends and must
address both content and process. In the final analysis, it does not really
matter whether those responsible for specifying learning tasks are called
'syllabus designers' or 'methodologists'. What matters is that both
processes and outcomes are taken care of and that there is a compatible
and creative relationship between the two.

Whatever the position taken, there is no doubt that the development of
communicative language teaching has had a profound effect on both
methodology and syllabus design, and has greatly enhanced the status of
the learning 'task' within the curriculum.

1.4   Curriculum development and learning tasks

'Curriculum' is a large and complex concept, and the term 'curriculum' is
used in a number of different ways. In some contexts it is used to refer to a
particular programme of study (for example the 'science curriculum' or
the 'mathematics curriculum'). In other contexts, it is used more widely. I
shall use 'syllabus' to refer to the selecting and grading of content, and
'curriculum' more widely to refer to all aspects of planning, implementing, evaluating and managing an educational programme (Nunan 1988).

Around forty years ago, Ralph Tyler suggested that a rational curriculum is developed by first identifying goals and objectives, then by listing,
organising and grading the learning experiences, and finally, by finding
means for determining whether the goals and objectives have been
achieved (Tyler 1949).

More recently, it has been suggested that at the very minimum a
curriculum should offer the following:

A. *In planning:*
   1. Principles for the selection of content – what is to be
      learned and taught.

2. Principles for the development of a teaching strategy – how it is to be learned and taught.
3. Principles for the making of decisions about sequence.
4. Principles on which to diagnose the strengths and weaknesses of individual students and differentiate the general principles 1, 2 and 3 above, to meet individual cases.

B. *In empirical study:*
   1. Principles on which to study and evaluate the progress of students.
   2. Principles on which to study and evaluate the progress of teachers.
   3. Guidance as to the feasibility of implementing the curriculum in varying school contexts, pupil contexts, environments and peer-group situations.
   4. Information about the variability of effects in differing contexts and on different pupils and an understanding of the causes of the variation.

C. *In relation to justification:*
   A formulation of the intention or aim of the curriculum which is accessible to critical scrutiny.

(Stenhouse 1975: 5)

This rather imposing (although by no means exhaustive) list serves to demonstrate just how comprehensive the field of curriculum study can be.

Turning more specifically to language teaching, the distinction traditionally drawn between syllabus design and methodology suggests that syllabus design deals with the selection and grading of content, while methodology is concerned with the selection and sequencing of learning activities. If one sticks to the traditional distinction, then task design would seem to belong to the realm of methodology. However, with the development of communicative language teaching, as I have indicated, the distinction between syllabus design and methodology becomes difficult to sustain: one needs not only to specify both the content (or ends of learning) and the tasks (or means to those ends) but also to integrate them. This suggests a broad perspective on curriculum in which concurrent consideration is given to content, methodology and evaluation.

Within this perspective, I make one substantial departure from the 'traditional' approach to curriculum design. With a traditional approach, such as the one suggested by Tyler, the curriculum designer first decides on the goals and objectives of instruction. Once these have been satisfactorily specified, the curriculum content is specified. The learning experiences are then decided upon, and, finally, the means for assessing learners and evaluating the curriculum are established. The process is

15

thus a linear one which operates in one direction, with a feedback loop from evaluation to goals as the following diagram shows:

Goals ⟶ Content ⟶ Experiences (Tasks) ⟶ Evaluation

Applying this to language curricula, one would first decide on why one's learners are coming along to learn in the first place. This would provide a rationale for the specification of grammatical items, functions, notions topics and so on. The learning experiences (or, as we are calling them, tasks) would be specified. Finally, means would be established for deciding whether the content has been learned and the goals achieved. This final evaluative step would allow us to decide whether our goals, content and tasks need to be modified.

But while this might seem to be a logical way of designing a curriculum, in practice it can be unnecessarily rigid: a more flexible approach, in which content and tasks are developed in tandem, generally leads to a more satisfactory and coherent end product. Taking a set of curriculum goals as our point of departure, we simultaneously specify content and develop learning tasks. We might illustrate such a process as follows:

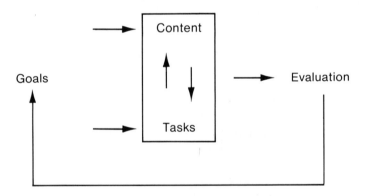

In this model, content and tasks are developed in tandem so that content can suggest tasks and vice versa. There is also a feedback loop so that the results of the evaluation can be fed back into the curriculum planning process.

The following example should serve to exemplify this process.

Imagine we are developing a curriculum for second language learners who want to study in English at university. Such a curriculum will have the following sorts of goals:

- Reading academic texts
- Taking part in tutorial discussions
- Obtaining and recording information from academic lectures
- Writing formal essays

In developing a unit of work for a goal such as 'reading academic texts' we might have as resources a number of syllabus checklists which specify topics, grammar, vocabulary etc. and input data in the form of a variety of reading texts and extracts. We would examine a given text and decide on an activity or sequence of activities requiring the learner to extract and transform the key information contained in the text in some way (for example, by completing a diagram). We would also determine which aspects of the content learners would need to engage in to complete the task successfully. This might include finding the meaning of a range of vocabulary items, comprehending logical relationships, identifying anaphoric links and understanding relative clauses. Separate exercises would be written for these, and the items would be checked off against our syllabus checklists. In this way, the syllabus would evolve in the course of preparing the programme, rather than preceding the specification of learning tasks and other exercise types.

So far I have described the curriculum process from the perspective of the curriculum or syllabus designer. Such people usually work at a more general or abstract level than those actually responsible for developing teaching materials, or for the day-to-day task of teaching. Classroom teachers, for instance, are generally presented with curriculum guidelines or sets of syllabus specifications, and are required to develop their courses and programmes from these. As their immediate focus is on the day-to-day schedule of work with learners in classrooms, their conception of tasks is somewhat different from that presented above. They tend to see lessons or units of work as the basic building blocks of their programmes. These lessons and units in turn are composed of sets of more or less integrated tasks and manipulative exercises of various sorts. The teacher's immediate preoccupation is thus with learning tasks and with integrating these into lessons and/or units (Nunan 1987; Shavelson and Stern 1981).

For the classroom teacher, then, a planning framework is likely to look something like the following:

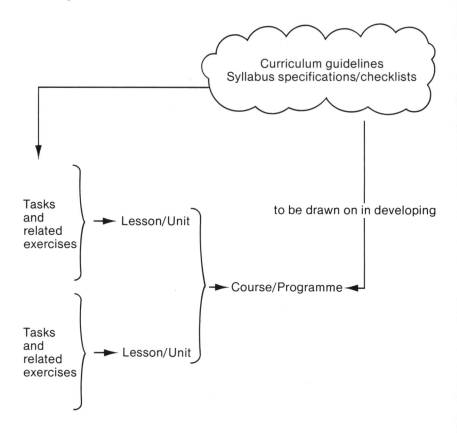

The notion of task therefore has an immediate relevancy, and planning for the teacher is a matter of putting tasks together, whatever the more general 'syllabus' or 'curriculum' sets out. Thus, while curriculum designers are more likely to take a long-term perspective, setting out plans for semesters and years, teachers and materials writers more often do their detailed planning in relation to lessons or units of work. In Chapter 6, we shall look at various ways in which chains of tasks can be integrated and sequenced to form coherent units of work.

> At this point, you might like to pause and reflect on the way the notion of 'task', as already described, fits into the scheme of things in your own situation as teacher, programme planner or course designer. Which of the diagrams set out in this section corresponds most closely to your own view? Which 'unit' of organisation do you regularly build your work around?

I am not trying to suggest that there is no longer any place for syllabus specifications as traditionally conceived, but rather that their place in the design process takes on a rather different function. Rather than working from syllabus items to tasks, I see syllabus specifications as traditionally conceived (i.e. lists of content) as being of most value as checklists and frameworks which can provide coherence and continuity to the course design and materials development process. For example, one might be developing materials for a 200-hour beginner's course. The syllabus (which will be used by the examiners to set an end-of-course examination) specifies sets of grammatical, phonological, lexical, functional and notional items to be covered. Rather than identifying a particular item, say 'talking about oneself', 'nationalities' and the verb 'be', and creating a text and a task to teach these items, one might find or create an interesting/relevant text and task at the appropriate level of difficulty, and then identify which language items on the syllabus checklist can be introduced or taught through the text/task. The course designer/ materials writer's task is thus to carry out a delicate juggling act between the various curriculum components, including sets of syllabus specifications, task and activity types, texts and input data.

1.5 The role of the learner

So far, we have considered how within CLT course designers and teachers might make use of the notion of task. Another trend in recent years which has stemmed from CLT has been the development of learner-centred approaches to language teaching, in which information by and from learners is used in planning, implementing and evaluating language programmes. While the learner-centred curriculum will contain similar elements and processes to traditional curricula, a key difference will be that information by and from learners will be built into every phase of the curriculum process. Curriculum development becomes a collaborative effort between teachers and learners, since learners will be involved in decisions on content selection, methodology and evaluation (Nunan 1988).

> Of course, no curriculum will ever be totally subject-centred or totally learner-centred. However, even within institutions in which teachers and learners have minimal input into the curriculum development process it is possible to introduce elements of learner-centredness. It is worth considering the ways in which your curriculum might be modified to make it more learner-centred.

The philosophical reasons for adopting a learner-centred approach to teaching have been reinforced by research into second language acquisition as well as work in the area of learning styles (Willing 1988).

Breen, who has written a great deal on learner-centred language teaching, has pointed out the advantages of linking learner-centredness with learning tasks. He draws attention to the frequent disparity between what the teacher intends as the outcome of a task and what the learners actually derive from it. (We may parallel this with a similar disparity between what curriculum documents say ought to happen, and what actually happens in the classroom.) Learning outcomes will be influenced by learners' perceptions about what they should contribute, their views about the nature and demands of the task, and their definitions of the situation in which the task takes place. Additionally, we cannot know for certain how different learners are likely to carry out a task. We tend to assume that the way we look at a task will be the way learners look at it. However, there is evidence that while we as teachers are focusing on one thing, learners are focusing on something else. How can we be sure, then, that learners will not look for grammatical patterns when taking part in activities which were designed to focus them on meaning, and look for meaning in tasks designed to focus them on grammatical forms?

One way of dealing with this tendency is to involve learners in designing or selecting tasks. It should also be possible to allow learners choices in deciding what to do and how to do it. This of course implies a major change in the roles assigned to learners and teachers. Here I am suggesting that the task is likely to have the same psychological/operational reality for the learner as it has for the teacher. By using it as a design unit, one opens to the student the possibility of planning and monitoring learning – one breaks down the hierarchic barriers as it were. This is not to say that the teacher and learner will view the same task in the same way and attach the same 'meanings' to it. Nor does it absolve the teacher from the responsibility of ensuring that through a sequence of tasks the appropriate 'formal curricula' are covered. These are issues of teacher and learner roles to which we shall return in Chapter 4.

1.6 Conclusion

In this chapter, I have introduced and defined 'task' in relation to the general field of language curriculum design. I have attempted to spell out some of the relationships between the concepts of curriculum, syllabus, methodology and task. I have suggested that tasks can be analysed in terms of their goals, input data, activities, settings and roles. I have tried to demonstrate how tasks can be used as building blocks in developing lessons and units of work, and how this development can proceed through the simultaneous specification of content and tasks. Finally, I have tried to indicate that the notion of task seems to be one to which teachers and learners can relate.

In the next chapter, we shall look in greater detail at the nature of communicative language learning and use from the perspective of the macroskills of listening, speaking, reading and writing. In particular, we shall consider how what we know about the macroskills can be incorporated into task design.

References and further reading

Breen, M. 1984. Processes in syllabus design. In C. Brumfit (Ed.) *General English Syllabus Design*. Oxford: Pergamon Press.

Breen, M. 1987. Learner contributions to task design. In C. Candlin and D. Murphy (Eds.) *Language Learning Tasks*. Englewood Cliffs NJ: Prentice-Hall.

Littlewood, W. 1981. *Communicative Language Teaching: An Introduction*. Cambridge: Cambridge University Press.

Long, M. 1985. A role for instruction in second language acquisition. In K. Hyltenstam and M. Pienemann (Eds.) *Modelling and Assessing Second Language Acquisition*. Clevedon Avon: Multilingual Matters.

Maley, A., and S. Moulding. 1981. *Learning to Listen*. Cambridge: Cambridge University Press.

Nunan, D. 1987. *The Teacher as Curriculum Developer*. Adelaide: National Curriculum Resource Centre.

Nunan, D. 1988. *The Learner-Centred Curriculum*. Cambridge: Cambridge University Press.

Richards, J., J. Platt, and H. Weber. 1986. *Longman Dictionary of Applied Linguistics*. London: Longman.

Shavelson, R. J., and Stern, P. 1981. Research on teachers' pedagogical thoughts, judgements, decisions and behaviour. *Review of Educational Research* 51, 4.

Stenhouse, L. 1975. *An Introduction to Curriculum Research and Development*. London: Heinemann.

Tyler, R. 1949. *Basic Principles of Curriculum and Instruction*. New York: Harcourt Brace.

Willing, K. 1988. *Learning Styles in Adult Migrant Education*. Adelaide: National Curriculum Resource Centre.

2 Analysing language skills

2.1 Introduction

Before we proceed, in Chapter 3, to consider in more detail the components of a language learning task, we need to draw together what we know about language use. We shall do this by looking at recent research into the nature of what we may call the four macroskills of listening, speaking, reading and writing.

We have already noted that a conventional approach to syllabus design has been to produce specifications or inventories of discrete linguistic items to build into composite items in the learning programme. These specifications have variously taken the shape of lists of forms, or functions, or notions, or particular skills. It is the last of these categories, with its emphasis on language behaviour, which we shall find most useful in helping us to chart those language activities which will help us make up our language learning tasks.

When in Chapter 3 we construct a framework for designing and monitoring tasks, we shall be considering all the skills conjointly as they interact with each other in natural behaviour. In real life as in the classroom, most tasks of any complexity involve more than one macroskill. There are occasions, certainly, when one is simply listening, speaking, reading or writing to the exclusion of the other skills: examples might be watching a soap opera on television, reading a novel, giving a lecture, or writing a letter to a friend. But there are many other examples where a number of skills are interwoven into a complex language activity. I would like us therefore to get away from the notion that general language programmes can be constructed from separate components concentrating on separate macroskills. Where possible these skills should be integrated, though this is not to say that there cannot be specialised components focusing on one or two of the skills to the exclusion of others.

Nevertheless, for convenience our starting point in this chapter is the discrete macroskills and what research has shown us about each of them in turn. We will consider later in the chapter such issues of syllabus design as when for classroom purposes we integrate skills and when we deal with them separately, and how we relate them to the aims of the learner and the goals of the programme.

2.2   The nature of listening comprehension

In their book on listening, Anderson and Lynch (1988) distinguish between reciprocal listening and non-reciprocal listening. Reciprocal listening refers to those listening tasks where there is the opportunity for the listener to interact with the speaker, and to negotiate the content of the interaction. Non-reciprocal listening refers to tasks such as listening to the radio or a formal lecture where the transfer of information is in one direction only – from the speaker to the listener. Anderson and Lynch underline the complexity of listening comprehension by pointing out that the listener must simultaneously integrate the following skills:

– identify spoken signals from the midst of surrounding sounds;
– segment the stream of speech into words;
– grasp the syntax of the utterance(s);
– (in interactive listening) formulate an appropriate response.

They point out that in addition to these linguistic skills, the listener must also command a range of non-linguistic knowledge and skills. These include having an appropriate purpose for listening; having appropriate social and cultural knowledge and skills; having the appropriate background knowledge. They stress the active nature of listening, and demonstrate the inadequate nature of the 'listener as tape-recorder' view of listening comprehension. We do not simply take language in like a tape-recorder, but interpret what we hear according to our purpose in listening and our background knowledge. We then store the meaning(s) of the message rather than the forms in which these are encoded. The actual grammatical structures themselves are often rapidly lost. Conversely, being able to remember the actual words of a spoken message does not necessarily mean that the message itself has been comprehended.

Anderson and Lynch record an anecdote which illustrates the importance of background knowledge. An old woman, passing one of the authors in the street, said 'That's the university. It's going to rain tomorrow.' Initially, the listener was unable to interpret the utterance. It was only after the speaker repeated herself, and drew the listener's attention to a bell ringing in the distance, that he was able to get to the meanings behind the words. In doing so, he needed to draw on the following information:

> *general factual information:*
> 1. sound is more audible downwind than upwind
> 2. wind direction may affect weather conditions
>
> *local factual knowledge:*
> 3. the University of Glasgow has a clock tower with a bell

socio-cultural knowledge:
4. strangers in Britain occasionally refer to the weather to 'oil the wheels' of social life.
5. a polite comment from a stranger usually requires a response

knowledge of context:
6. the conversation took place about half-a-mile from the University of Glasgow
7. the clock tower bell was just striking the hour

(Anderson and Lynch 1988: 12–13)

By drawing on these various sources of knowledge, the listener was able to conclude that the old woman was drawing his attention to the fact that the wind was blowing from a direction which brought with it the threat of rain. The change in the wind direction was signalled by the fact that the university clock tower was audible. The woman was, in fact, making a socially acceptable comment to a stranger, i.e. talking about the weather, although she chose a rather idiosyncratic way of doing it.

In his analysis of listening comprehension, Richards (1987a) distinguishes between conversational listening (listening to casual speech) and academic listening (listening to lectures and other academic presentations). (By 'academic' listening Richards means listening to lectures in an academic context, not an English language learning context.)

Conversational listening involves the ability to:

- retain chunks of language of different lengths for short periods
- discriminate among the distinctive sounds of the target language
- recognise the stress patterns of words
- recognise the rhythmic structure of English
- recognise the functions of stress and intonation to signal the information structure of utterances
- identify words in stressed and unstressed positions
- recognise reduced forms of words
- distinguish word boundaries
- recognise typical word order patterns in the target language
- recognise vocabulary used in core conversational topics
- detect key words (i.e. those which identify topics and propositions)
- guess the meanings of words from the contexts in which they occur
- recognise grammatical word classes (parts of speech)
- recognise major syntactic patterns and devices
- recognise cohesive devices in spoken discourse
- recognise elliptical forms of grammatical units and sentences
- detect sentence constituents.

Academic listening involves the ability to:

- identify purpose and scope of lecture
- identify topic of lecture and follow topic development
- identify relationships among units within discourse (for example major idea, generalisations, hypotheses, supporting ideas, examples)
- identify role of discourse markers in signalling structure of lecture (for example conjunctions, adverbs, gambits, routines)
- infer relationships (for example cause, effect, conclusion)
- recognise key lexical items relating to subject/topic
- deduce meanings of words from context
- recognise markers of cohesion
- recognise function of intonation to signal information structure (for example pitch, volume, pace, key)
- detect attitude of speaker toward subject matter.

> Study these and decide which are likely to be carried out by the learner in the world outside the language classroom, which are only likely to occur in the classroom, and which might occur both inside and outside the language classroom.

Rather than seeing these lists as relating to conversational and academic listening respectively, I would prefer to suggest that the first list contains a set of enabling microskills which learners might employ in any listening task regardless of whether it is a conversational or academic task. The second list contains what might be called rhetorical or discourse comprehension skills. Once again, these may be needed for both conversational and academic listening.

Richards also classifies listening tasks according to whether they require the learner to engage in 'bottom-up' or 'top-down' processing. Bottom-up processes work on the incoming message itself, decoding sounds, words, clauses and sentences. Bottom-up processes include the following:

- scanning the input to identify familiar lexical items;
- segmenting the stream of speech into constituents, for example in order to recognise that 'abookofmine' consists of four words;
- using phonological cues to identify the information focus in an utterance;
- using grammatical cues to organise the input into constituents, for example, in order to recognise that in 'the book which I lent you' [the book] and [which I lent you] are major constituents, rather than [the book which I] and [lent you].

Top-down processes use background knowledge to assist in comprehending the message. (We have already seen, through the example provided by Anderson and Lynch, the importance of top-down processes in listening comprehension.) Richards provides the following examples:

- assigning an interaction to part of a particular event, such as story telling, joking, praying, complaining;
- assigning places, persons or things to categories;
- inferring cause and effect relationships;
- anticipating outcomes;
- inferring the topic of a discourse;
- inferring the sequence between events;
- inferring missing details.

In addition to the 'bottom-up/top-down' processing dimension, Richards suggests that there is also a functional dimension. Following Brown and Yule (1983), to whom we shall return in 2.3, he distinguishes between functions which are interactional and those which are transactional. In the next section, we shall consider this distinction in relation to the speaking skill.

In summary, then, let us note that successful listening involves:

- skills in segmenting the stream of speech into meaningful words and phrases;
- recognising word classes;
- relating the incoming message to one's own background knowledge;
- identifying the rhetorical and functional intent of an utterance or parts of an aural text;
- interpreting rhythm, stress and intonation to identify information focus and emotional/attitudinal tone;
- extracting gist/essential information from longer aural texts without necessarily understanding every word.

2.3 The nature of speaking and oral interaction

Brown and Yule (1983) begin their discussion on the nature of spoken language by distinguishing between spoken and written language. They point out that for most of its history, language teaching has been concerned with the teaching of written language. This language is characterised by well-formed sentences which are integrated into highly structured paragraphs. Spoken language, on the other hand, consists of short, often fragmentary utterances, in a range of pronunciations. There is often a great deal of repetition and overlap between one speaker and another, and speakers frequently use non-specific references (they tend to say 'thing', 'it' and 'this' rather than 'the left-handed monkey wrench', or 'the highly perfumed French poodle on the sofa'). Brown and Yule point out that the loosely organised syntax, the use of non-specific words and phrases and the use of fillers such as 'well', 'oh' and 'uhuh' make spoken language feel less conceptually dense than other types of language such as expository prose. They suggest that, in contrast with the teaching of written language, teachers concerned with teaching the spoken language must confront the following types of questions:

- What is the appropriate form of spoken language to teach?
- From the point of view of pronunciation, what is a reasonable model?
- How important is pronunciation?
- Is it any more important than teaching appropriate handwriting in the foreign language?
- If so, why?
- From the point of view of the structures taught, is it all right to teach the spoken language as if it were exactly like the written language, but with a few 'spoken expressions' thrown in?
- Is it appropriate to teach the same structures to all foreign language students, no matter what their age is or their intentions in learning the spoken language?
- Are those structures which are described in standard grammars the structures which our students should be expected to produce when they speak English?
- How is it possible to give students any sort of meaningful practice in producing spoken English?

(Brown and Yule 1983: 3)

Brown and Yule also draw a useful distinction between two basic language functions. These are the transactional function, which is primarily concerned with the transfer of information, and the inter-actional function, in which the primary purpose of speech is the mainten-ance of social relationships.

Another basic distinction we can make when considering the develop-ment of speaking skills is between monologue and dialogue. The ability to give an uninterrupted oral presentation is quite distinct from inter-acting with one or more other speakers for transactional and inter-actional purposes. While all native speakers can and do use language interactionally, not all native speakers have the ability to extemporise on a given subject to a group of listeners. This is a skill which generally has to be learned and practised. Brown and Yule suggest that most language teaching is concerned with developing skills in short, interactional exchanges in which the learner is only required to make one or two utterances at a time. They go on to state that:

> . . . the teacher should realise that simply training the student to produce short turns will not automatically yield a student who can perform satisfactorily in long turns. It is currently fashionable in language teaching to pay particular attention to the forms and functions of short turns. . . . It must surely be clear that students who are only capable of producing short turns are going to experience a lot of frustration when they try to speak the foreign language.

(Brown and Yule 1983: 19–20)

Do you agree with this conclusion? To what extent is it feasible or desirable for your own students to develop skills in giving extended oral presentations?

Many of the insights of research into first language development have relevance for the learning of a second language, as is shown by Wells (1981). He provides the following conversational extract between a 28-month-old child and his mother.

Table 1.1. *A conversation between a child and his mother*

1 Mark: Play Mummy(v)		
2	Mother: All right	
3 Mark: [ʃɪʃ] wash up Mummy(v)? (= have you finished washing up?)		
4	Mother: Pardon?	
5 Mark: [ʃɪʃ] wash up?		
6	Mother: Yes	
7 Mark: Oh		
8	Mother: Let me just dry my hands	
9 Mark: Alright		
10 In there		[Mark looks for towel]
11	Mother: Here	
12 Mark: [ɪəɑ] (= here you are)		[Mark gives towel to Mother]
13	Mother: Just a minute	
14	Will you put the top back on the washing basket please	
15 Mark: Uh?		

16		Uh?	
17		Mother:	Put the top back on the wash-ing basket
18	Mark:	On there Mummy(v)?	
19		On there?	
20		Mother:	Yes
21		Mother:	No not the towel in there
22			The top of the basket on it
23	Mark:	Alright	
24	Mark:	On there	
25		Uh?	
26		Uh?	
27		Mother:	Put the lid . . . on top of the basket
28	Mark:	On er-on there?	
29		Mother:	Yes please
30	Mark:	Alright	
31		You dry hands	
32		Mother:	I've dried my hands now
33	Mark:	Put towel in there	
34		Mother:	No it's not dirty
35	Mark:	Tis	
36		Mother:	No it isn't
37	Mark:	Tis	
38		Mummy(v) play	
39		Play Mummy(v)	
40		Mother:	Well I will play if you put the top on the basket
41	Mark:	Alright	
42		There	[Mark puts top on basket]
43		There	
44		Play Mummy(v)	
45		Mummy(v) come on	

Wells: Learning through Interaction, pp. 24–5

According to Wells, this extract shows that the child, Mark, has success-fully developed interactional skills. He knows when it is his turn to speak, he is able to relate his own utterances to his mother's previous turns, and he is able to systematically relate his conversation to the physical situation in which it occurs. Despite these skills, his lack of linguistic maturity is obvious.

The interactional nature of spoken language is examined by Bygate (1987). He distinguishes between motor-perceptive skills, which are concerned with correctly using the sounds and structures of the language, and interactional skills, which involve using motor-perceptive skills for the purposes of communication. Motor-perceptive skills are developed in the language classroom through activities such as model dialogues, pattern practice, oral drills and so on. Until relatively recently, it was assumed that mastery of motor-perceptive skills was all that one needed in order to communicate successfully. We now know that this is not necessarily the case, and that learners can benefit from direct classroom practice in communicative interaction. Bygate suggests that, in particular, learners need to develop skills in the management of interaction and also in the negotiation of meaning. The management of interaction involves such things as knowing when and how to take the floor, when to introduce a topic or change the subject, how to invite someone else to speak, how to keep a conversation going, when and how to terminate the conversation and so on. Negotiation of meaning refers to the skill of making sure the person you are speaking to has correctly understood you and that you have correctly understood them (making sure, in other words, that you are both 'on about' the same thing).

Like Bygate, Pattison (1987) is concerned with the lack of transfer from the practice of motor-perceptive skills to genuine communicative interaction. She contrasts what conventionally happens in the language class with what typically happens outside the classroom in relation to the content, reason, result, participants and means of communication. The contrasts are as follows:

List 1 FL (oral) *practice in the classroom*	*List 2 FL (oral)* *communication outside the classroom*
WHAT: *Content of communication*	
Content or topic is decided by teacher, textbook, tape, etc. The meaning of what they say may not always be clear to the speakers. The content is highly predictable.	Speakers express their own ideas, wishes, opinions, attitudes, information, etc. They are fully aware of the meaning they wish to convey. The exact content of any speaker's message is unpredictable.

WHY 1: *Reason for communication*

Learners speak in order to practise speaking; because teacher tells them to; in order to get a good mark, etc.	Speakers have a social or personal reason to speak. There is an information gap to be filled, or an area of uncertainty to be made clear. What is said is potentially interesting or useful to the participants.

WHY 2: *Result of communication*

The FL is spoken; the teacher accepts or corrects what is said; a mark is given, etc. (extrinsic motivation).	Speakers achieve their aims; they get what they wanted, an information gap is filled, a problem is solved, a decision is reached or a social contact is made, etc. The result is of intrinsic interest or value to the participants.

WHO: *Participants in communication*

A large group in which not everyone is facing the speakers or interested in what they say; except for one person, the teacher, who pays less attention to what they say than to how correctly they say it.	Two or more people, usually facing each other, paying attention and responding to what is said, rather than to how correctly it is said.

HOW: *Means of communication*

Language from teacher or tape is very closely adapted to learners' level. All speech is as accurate as possible, and usually in complete sentences. Problems in communicating meaning are often dealt with by translation. Learners are corrected if their speech deviates from standard forms, whether or not their meaning is clear. Teachers help learners to express themselves more correctly.	Native-speaker output is not very closely adjusted to foreigners' level. Meaning is conveyed by any means at the speakers' command: linguistic or para-linguistic (gestures, etc.). Problems are dealt with by negotiation and exchange of feedback between speakers. Translation is not always possible. Errors not affecting communication are largely ignored. Native speakers help foreign speakers to express themselves more clearly.

Pattison: Developing Communication Skills, pp. 7 and 8

Pattison then considers a range of strategies for making classroom practice more closely resemble communication outside the classroom.

> You might like to examine a selection of speaking tasks from your own classroom and consider the extent to which these resemble communication outside the classroom. Would it be feasible or desirable to try and make your classroom tasks resemble more closely out-of-class communication?

Finally, we can apply to speaking the bottom-up/top-down distinction which we introduced in the last section. The bottom-up approach to speaking suggests that we start with the smallest units of language, i.e. individual sounds, and move through mastery of words and sentences to discourse. The top-down view, on the other hand, suggests that we start with the larger chunks of language, which are embedded in meaningful contexts, and use our knowledge of these contexts to comprehend and use correctly the smaller elements of language. Proponents of a top-down view of language development suggest that, rather than teaching learners to make well-formed sentences and then putting these to use in discourse, we should encourage learners to take part in discourse, and through discourse, help them to master sentences.

In summary then, successful oral communication involves developing:

– the ability to articulate phonological features of the language comprehensibly;
– mastery of stress, rhythm, intonation patterns;
– an acceptable degree of fluency;
– transactional and interpersonal skills;
– skills in taking short and long speaking turns;
– skills in the management of interaction;
– skills in negotiating meaning;
– conversational listening skills (successful conversations require good listeners as well as good speakers);
– skills in knowing about and negotiating purposes for conversations;
– using appropriate conversational formulae and fillers.

2.4   The nature of reading comprehension

Having looked at bottom-up and top-down approaches to listening comprehension, we can now apply the concepts to the analysis of reading comprehension. With the bottom-up approach, reading is viewed as a process of decoding written symbols, working from smaller units (individual letters) to larger ones (words, clauses and sentences). In other words, we use strategies to decode written forms in order to arrive at meaning.

The bottom-up approach to reading has come in for some rather severe criticism over the years. Smith (1978), in fact, argues that reading actually works in the reverse order from that proposed by the bottom-up approach. In other words, that we need to comprehend meanings in order to identify words, and that we generally need to identify words in order to identify letters.

More recent research indicates that both bottom-up decoding strategies and top-down strategies may be used in learning to read, and that efficient reading may require the integration of both bottom-up and top-down strategies (Stanovich 1980).

Schema theory and reading

One significant contribution to reading provided by the top-down school has been to show the importance of background knowledge to the reading process. We saw in Section 2.2 the importance of background knowledge to listening, and the same holds for reading. The mental structures which store our knowledge are called schemata, and the theory of comprehension based on schemata is called schema theory. According to the theory, reading is an interactive process between what a reader already knows about a given topic or subject and what the writer writes. It is not simply a matter of applying decoding conventions and grammatical knowledge to the text. Good readers are able to relate the text and their own background knowledge efficiently.

Schema theory is particularly significant for second language learners. Many reading passages can only be adequately comprehended if the reader has the relevant cultural knowledge. Nunan (1984) found that, for high school ESL readers, relevant background knowledge was a more important factor in reading comprehension than grammatical complexity. (See also the papers in Carrell *et al.* 1988.)

Reading skills and reader purpose

It is important to bear in mind that reading is not an invariant skill, that there are different types of reading skills which correspond to the many different purposes we have for reading.

Rivers and Temperley suggest that second language learners will want to read for the following purposes:

1. to obtain information for some purpose or because we are curious about some topic
2. to obtain instructions on how to perform some task for our work or daily life (e.g. knowing how an appliance works)
3. to act in a play, play a game, do a puzzle.
4. to keep in touch with friends by correspondence or to understand business letters
5. to know when or where something will take place or what is available
6. to know what is happening or has happened (as reported in newspapers, magazines, reports)
7. for enjoyment or excitement

(Adapted from Rivers and Temperley 1978: 187–8)

> Which of these purposes are likely to be relevant for your own learners? Do these different purposes require different skills? If so, can you suggest what these are?

Consider the different reading skills required to carry out the following everyday, non-specialist tasks:

- filling in an unfamiliar form
- receiving an unfamiliar cheque and wanting to process it through a bank
- making an emergency call to a hospital
- operating a vending machine you have never used before
- finding a Telecom card under the door
- dealing with a note brought home from your child's school
- contacting a tradesman to do some work in your home
- looking in a newspaper to find a flat to rent
- interpreting labels on pharmaceutical products
- shopping for a particular product, for example dishwashing detergent
- using a timetable
- using road signs
- selecting and reading a newspaper article
- reading a short story or novel

These tasks have been taken from Brosnan *et al.* 1984. They make suggestions about what is involved in each of these reading tasks. For example, when your child brings a note home from school, you might:

- glance over it noting script, style and format;
- skim over it picking up key words and information (who it is from, the date etc.);

- on the basis of the above, anticipate the content and purpose;
- skim again, disregarding unimportant parts;
- read again in more detail, checking you have all the information;
- respond by ringing or writing a note to the teacher;
- keep the note for further reference.

In carrying out the reading task, you would have been involved in:

- recognising and understanding script and format;
- recognising and understanding key words and phrases;
- skimming for gist;
- identifying the main points in text;
- reading in detail.

(Brosnan *et al.* 1984: 29)

> To what extent does your own reading programme teach these skills? Are there any skills which, in your opinion, Brosnan *et al.* have left out?

Successful reading, then, involves:

- using word attack skills such as identifying sound/symbol correspondences;
- using grammatical knowledge to recover meaning, for example interpreting non-finite clauses;
- using different techniques for different purposes, for example skimming and scanning for key words or information;
- relating text content to one's own background knowledge of the subject at hand;
- identifying the rhetorical or functional intention of individual sentences or text segments, for example recognising when the writer is offering a definition or a summary even when these are not explicitly signalled by phrases such as 'X may be defined as . . . '.

2.5 The nature of writing

It has been argued that learning to write fluently and expressively is the most difficult of the macroskills for all language users regardless of whether the language in question is a first, second or foreign language. All children, except those with physiological disabilities, learn to comprehend and speak their native language. Not all of these learn to read. Fewer still learn to write fluently and legibly. White puts it this way:

> Writing is not a natural activity. All physically and mentally
> normal people learn to speak a language. Yet all people have to be
> taught how to write. This is a crucial difference between the
> spoken and written forms of language. There are other important
> differences as well. Writing, unlike speech, is displaced in time.
> Indeed, this must be one reason why writing originally evolved
> since it makes possible the transmission of a message from one
> place to another. A written message can be received, stored and
> referred back to at any time. It is permanent in comparison with
> the ephemeral 'here one minute and gone the next' character of
> spoken language – even of spoken language that is recorded on
> tape or disk.

(White 1981:2)

Bell and Burnaby (1984) point out that writing is an extremely complex
cognitive activity in which the writer is required to demonstrate control
of a number of variables simultaneously. At the sentence level these
include control of content, format, sentence structure, vocabulary,
punctuation, spelling and letter formation. Beyond the sentence, the
writer must be able to structure and integrate information into cohesive
and coherent paragraphs and texts.

In recent years, two different views on the nature of writing have
emerged. The first of these is what we can call the product approach. The
second we shall call the process approach.

The product approach to writing focuses on the end result of the act of
composition, i.e. the letter, essay, story and so on. The writing teacher
who subscribes to the product approach will be concerned to see that the
end product is readable, grammatically correct and obeys discourse
conventions relating to main points, supporting details and so on. The
focus in class will be on copying and imitation, carrying out sentence
expansions from cue words and developing sentences and paragraphs
from models of various sorts.

Those who advocate a process approach to writing see the act of
composition from a very different perspective, focusing as much on the
means whereby the completed text was created as on the end product
itself. In order to find out more about how writers arrive at their final
product, researchers studied writers as they went about their work. One
of the most important discoveries, according to Zamel (1982), was that
the act of composing evolves through several stages as writers discover,
through the process, what it is that they are trying to say. In other words,
one does not sit down and simply record, in a linear fashion, what it is
that one wants to say. In many instances, the writer starts out with only
the vaguest notion of this. The ideas are then refined, developed and
transformed as the writer writes and rewrites.

36

> Do you sympathise with the process or product approach? Are they incompatible?

Researchers have also studied skilled and unskilled writers in order to find out which strategies seemed to be most successful. Sommers and Perl (cited in Zamel 1982) found some significant differences between skilled and unskilled writers.

> . . . less skilled writers, who view composing as more mechanical and formulaic, are so inhibited by their concerns with correctness and form that they cannot get beyond the surface in order to anticipate the needs and expectations of their readers.
>
> . . . less skilled writers revised in the most limited way; they were basically concerned with lexicon and teacher-generated rules and rarely modified ideas that had already been written down.
>
> . . . Unlike these writers, the more experienced writers observed by Sommers viewed their writing from a more global perspective. In the process of discovering meaning, these experienced writers changed whole chunks of discourse, and each of these changes represented a reordering of the whole.
>
> (Zamel 1982:195–209)

> What school of thought does this extract represent – process or product?

Successful writing then involves:

– mastering the mechanics of letter formation;
– mastering and obeying conventions of spelling and punctuation;
– using the grammatical system to convey one's intended meaning;
– organising content at the level of the paragraph and the complete text to reflect given/new information and topic/comment structures;
– polishing and revising one's initial efforts;
– selecting an appropriate style for one's audience.

2.6 Implications for task design

In this section, I shall attempt to draw together the major points to have emerged so far and spell out their implications for task design.

First of all, we have seen that there is a basic distinction between top-down and bottom-up approaches to language comprehension and production. Bottom-up approaches focus on the various components of the language and then fit these together in comprehending or producing language. Top-down approaches utilise knowledge of the larger picture, as it were, to assist in comprehending or using smaller elements.

In designing communicative language tasks, we need to consider the extent to which it is necessary to focus on linguistic form. Some language specialists (see, for example, Prabhu 1987) believe that it is not necessary to provide practice activities which focus on individual linguistic components as a preliminary to engagement in communicative tasks. They argue that involvement in communicative tasks is all that is necessary to develop competence in a second language. Others (for example, Rutherford 1987) believe that a linguistic focus, in the form of grammatical consciousness-raising activities, should be incorporated into task design.

While in some ways the top-down, bottom-up distinction corresponds to the distinction between form-focused and meaning-focused tasks, there is no one-to-one correspondence. For example, the listening task opposite, in which learners listen to a weather forecast and then carry out the task, is essentially a bottom-up one, in that the learner is only required to process isolated elements. Yet it could be argued that the learner's attention is focused as much on the meaning as the form.

Another major issue to emerge from our examination of the macroskills relates to the real-world uses the learner has for the target language. We saw that Brown and Yule (1983) distinguish between interactional and transactional tasks. They also differentiate between short and long speaking turns. Richards (1987a) distinguishes between conversational and academic listening. Rivers and Temperley (1978) list a range of purposes for reading in a second language.

This last point may prove a logical point of departure in designing a syllabus. The various uses which a learner has (or, in the case of some foreign language learners, might potentially have) for learning another language can be revealed through various forms of needs analysis. Tasks are then justified on the grounds that they will help the learner develop the skills they will need for carrying out real-world communicative tasks beyond the classroom.

But while this might seem terribly obvious or logical, there is controversy over the extent to which classroom tasks should be made to mirror real-world tasks. Some people believe classroom tasks should replicate real-world tasks, and that the best way to learn is by doing. Others say this is unnecessary, that classroom tasks can be justified on other grounds. We shall look at this debate in the next section.

Unit 2

Exercise 12. How many times can you hear these words?

Listen and Count

weather		
fine		
warm		

Exercise 13. How many times can you hear these words?

Listen and Count

hot		
mild		
sunny		

Exercise 14. How many times can you hear these words?

Listen and Count

temperature		
fine		

Answers p. 30

Forrester, Palmer and Spinks: It's Over to You, p. 18

39

2.7 Task rationale

As intimated in the preceding section, classroom tasks are generally justified or rationalised in either 'real-world' or 'pedagogic' terms. Tasks with a real-world rationale require learners to approximate, in class, the sorts of behaviours required of them in the world beyond the classroom. (The term 'real-world' is used here as a form of shorthand. It is not suggested that the classroom is not 'real'.) Tasks with a pedagogic rationale, on the other hand, require learners to do things which it is extremely unlikely they would be called upon to do outside the classroom. As they cannot be justified on the grounds that they are enabling learners to rehearse real-world behaviours, they must have an alternative rationale. This usually takes a psycholinguistic form along the lines of: 'Well, although the learners are engaged in tasks which they are unlikely to perform outside the classroom, the tasks are stimulating internal processes of acquisition.' Thus, while the selection of real-world tasks (as we shall call tasks with a real-world rationale) will proceed with reference to some form of needs analysis, pedagogic tasks will be selected with reference to some theory or model of second language acquisition.

The distinction being drawn here can be illustrated as follows:

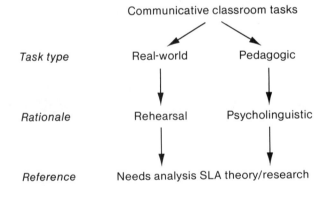

An example of a real-world task might be:

> The learner will listen to a weather forecast and identify the predicted maximum temperature for the day.
> *Or*
> The learner will listen to a weather forecast and decide whether or not to take an umbrella and sweater to school.

A pedagogic task might be:

> The learner will listen to an aural text and answer questions afterwards on whether given statements are true or false.

In fact, this distinction between real-world and pedagogic tasks is not hard and fast. Rather, it is a continuum. There will be some tasks which, though in principle authentic, are of such unlikely occurrence that the learner will come across them only in the classroom (for example, for younger children, 'Making a formal introduction'). There are some obviously pedagogic tasks for which it is possible to create real-life contexts (for example 'Listen to an aural text and write a sentence restating the gist.'). And there will be some tasks residing at the centre of the continuum which will be difficult to assign to one category or another (for example, 'Listen to the weather forecast for tomorrow and write a note to a friend telling about the weather.'). The distinction, nevertheless, is a powerful one.

Those who justify pedagogic tasks do so on the grounds that, while learners might not want to carry out those precise tasks in the real world, involvement in the tasks will provide them with skills for those real-world tasks which are difficult to predict in advance, or which are not feasible to practise in class. For example, the learner who has mastered the pedagogic task of listening to a news report about a terrorist attack in the Middle East and then completing yes/no questions which require them to distinguish between true and false inferences might be able to use the listening and thinking skills they have developed for comprehending radio and television news broadcasts outside the classroom.

In some language courses, on the other hand, all tasks are specified in real-world terms. Learners progress towards course goals by undertaking classroom activities which require them to practise repeatedly the target real-world activities. However, it is unusual for real-world tasks not to be modified or adapted in some way when they are brought into the classroom. For example, the interview could be re-recorded at a slower pace, the teacher might replay it several times, and the students might be given assistance in the form of three or four clues or suggestions rather than having to come up with the correct answer unaided. (In Chapter 5, we look in detail at the factors which can alter the difficulty of a task.)

Following Widdowson (1987), we might call the specification of tasks in real-world terms the 'rehearsal' approach to language development.

As we have seen, it is also possible to find tasks which do not at all resemble the things learners will need or want to be able to do outside the classroom. These may include non-communicative or pseudo-communicative activity types such as repetition, substitution and transformation drills. The justification for including these activities and exercises would be on the grounds that the tasks develop the necessary prerequisite skills required by learners for communicating in the target language (in the case of drills, the necessary fluency and mastery over structural and phonological patterns in the language).

There are also communicative tasks which have little real-world relevance but which have validity because they are none the less intellectually valid and meaning-focused and therefore put language to use, even though they engage learners in activities which are unlikely to occur in the world outside the classroom. Many of the tasks in the Bangalore Project would fall into this category. Prabhu, the principal architect of the Project, saw no need to link tasks to the real world.

> . . . a procedural syllabus of tasks only envisages constant effort by learners to deploy their language resources in the classroom, and does not attempt either to demarcate areas of real-life use for different stages of teaching or to bring about a 'thorough' learning of use in some functions at each stage.

(Prabhu 1987: 93)

Rather than being justified on the grounds of their real-world value, tasks in the Bangalore Project are justified on the grounds that they stimulate internal psycholinguistic processes of acquisition.

> Here is a list of tasks from the Bangalore Project. Where would you place them on the real-world/pedagogic continuum? How relevant are they, and in what ways, for your own learners?

Task Type	Examples
1. Diagrams and formations	– Naming parts of a diagram with numbers and letters of the alphabet as instructed. – Placing numbers and letters of the alphabet in given crossword formats.
2. Drawing	– Drawing geometrical figures/formations from sets of verbal instructions. – Comparing given figures to identify similarities and differences.
3. Clockfaces	– Telling the time from a clockface; positioning the hands of a clock to show a given time. – Stating the time on a twelve-hour clock and a twenty-four-hour clock.
4. Monthly calendar	– Calculating duration in days and weeks (in the context of travel, leave etc.).

5. Maps	– Finding, naming or describing specific locations on a given map.
	– Constructing the floor plan of a house from a description.
6. School timetables	– Constructing class timetables from instructions or descriptions.
	– Constructing timetables for teachers of particular subjects from given class timetables and vice versa.
7. Programmes and itineraries	– Constructing itineraries from descriptions of travel or from a statement of needs and intentions.
	– Working out feasible timings for personal appointments consistent with the requirements of work, travel etc.
8. Train timetables	– Interpreting train timetables.
	– Selecting trains appropriate to given needs.
9. Age and year of birth	– Working out year of birth from age.
	– Relating individuals' age/year of birth to given age requirements (e.g. school enrolment).
10. Money	– Working out the money needed to buy a set of things (e.g. school stationery, vegetables).
	– Deciding on quantities to be bought with the money available.
11. Tabular information	– Interpreting information presented in tables.
	– Constructing tables from given information.
12. Distances	– Working out the distances between places, from given distances between other places or from the scale of a map.
13. Rules	– Interpreting sets of rules e.g. those for concessional bus tickets for students.
	– Applying rules to given cases/situations.
14. The postal system	– Inferring the geographical location of places from their postal code numbers.
	– Deciding on the quickest way to send a

	letter, given a set of circumstances and the rules of the Quick Mail Service.
15. Telegrams	— Composing telegrams for given purposes, with the aim of reconciling economy with clarity.
16. Stories and dialogues	— Identifying factual inconsistencies in given narrative or descriptive accounts.
17. Classification	— Finding the 'odd man out' in a given set of objects or a classified list. — Making classified lists from unclassified ones.
18. Personal lists	— Finding items of information relevant to a particular situation in an individual's curriculum vitae.

(Adapted from Prabhu 1987: 138–43)

There is, in fact, a branch of classroom-centred research which has conducted some interesting investigations into the types of tasks likely to stimulate interactive language use. In an early study, Long *et al.* (1976) found that small-group work prompted students to use a greater range of language functions than whole-class activities. Doughty and Pica (1986) found that there was more negotiation of meaning in activities in which the exchange of information was essential (rather than optional) for the successful completion of the activity. Duff (1986) discovered that problem-solving tasks prompted more interaction than debating tasks. Varonis and Gass (1983) found that there was more modified interaction in small groups in which the learners were from different language backgrounds and proficiency levels. (For a detailed review of classroom studies see Chaudron, 1988.)

In fact, as I have already hinted, the distinction between real-world and pedagogic tasks may be more apparent than real. Many may be justified both in real-world and pedagogic terms. In Long's (1985) approach to course design, tasks start out as pedagogic, but gradually work towards the in-class simulation of real-world behaviours. Also, pedagogic activities (such as some problem-solving ones), while they may look artificial, particularly in terms of their content, may, on analysis, be practising enabling skills such as fluency, discourse and interactional skills, mastery of phonological elements and mastery of grammar. Thus, there is no reason, in principle, why skills developed in using wh-questions to complete a fictional family tree (a pedagogic task which, in all probability, the learner will never be required to perform in real life) might not be employed by the learner in the real world to obtain information from a neighbour or child's teacher.

In looking at claims for the inclusion of various sorts of real-world and pedagogic tasks in the language curriculum, we need to consider the extent to which classroom tasks can be expected to 'mirror' the real world. As I intimated earlier, it is unusual for real-world tasks not to be adapted in some way when they are brought into the classroom, and many real-world tasks are transformed into games, simulations, role plays and the like in order to make them appropriate for the classroom.

2.8 Conclusion

In this chapter, we have looked in detail at the skills which make up competence in a language. We have seen that some of these skills can be incorporated directly or indirectly into task design. Although we have looked at each macroskill separately we have noted that in normal behaviour they are frequently intertwined. We have looked at the interrelationship of broad features such as 'background knowledge' and narrow ones such as specific motor-perceptual skills. This has led us to explore the distinction between real-world and pedagogic tasks.

In the discussion it will have become apparent that it is difficult to separate clearly syllabus design issues from methodological ones, that we cannot discuss syllabus design without becoming engaged in questions of methodology and vice versa. In particular, methodological issues cannot be considered in isolation from the goals of a programme and the purposes of the learner. The next chapter discusses task components beginning with the goals which a task pursues.

References and further reading

Anderson, A., and T. Lynch. 1988. *Listening*. Oxford: Oxford University Press.
Bell, J., and B. Burnaby. 1984. *A Handbook for ESL Literacy*. Toronto: OISE.
Brosnan, D., K. Brown, and S. Hood. 1984. *Reading in Context*. Adelaide: National Curriculum Resource Centre.
Brown, G., and G. Yule. 1983. *Teaching the Spoken Language*. Cambridge: Cambridge University Press.
Bygate, M. 1987. *Speaking*. Oxford: Oxford University Press.
Carrell, P., J. Devine, and D. Eskey (Eds.) 1988. *Interactive Approaches to Second Language Reading*. Cambridge: Cambridge University Press.
Chaudron, C. 1988. *Second Language Classrooms: Research on Teaching and Learning*. Cambridge: Cambridge University Press.
Doughty, C., and T. Pica. 1986. 'Information gap' tasks: Do they facilitate second language acquisition? *TESOL Quarterly* 20 (2), 305–25.

Duff, P. 1986. Another look at interlanguage talk: Taking tasks to task. In R. Day (Ed.) *Talking to Learn*. Rowley Mass.: Newbury House.

Forrester, H., L. Palmer, and P. Spinks. 1986. *It's Over To You*. Adelaide: Department of Technical and Further Education.

Goodman, K. 1971. Psycholinguistic universals in the reading process. In P. Pimsleur and T. Quinn (Eds.) *The Psychology of Second Language Learning*. Cambridge: Cambridge University Press.

Long, M. 1985. A role for instruction in second language acquisition: Task-based language training. In K. Hyltenstam and M. Pienemann (Eds.) *Modelling and Assessing Second Language Acquisition*. Clevedon Avon: Multilingual Matters.

Long, M., L. Adams, and F. Castanos. 1976. Doing things with words: Verbal interaction in lockstep and small group classroom situations. In R. Crymes and J. Fanselow (Eds.) *On TESOL '76*. Washington DC: TESOL.

Nunan, D. 1984. Discourse processing by first language, second phase and second language learners. Unpublished doctoral dissertation. The Flinders University of South Australia.

Pattison, P. 1987. *Developing Communication Skills*. Cambridge: Cambridge University Press.

Perl, S. 1980. A look at basic writers in the process of composing. In L. Kasden, and D. Hoeber (Eds.) *Basic Writing*. Urbana Ill.: National Council of Teachers of English.

Prabhu, N. 1987. *Second Language Pedagogy: A Perspective*. Oxford: Oxford University Press.

Richards, J. 1987a. Designing instructional materials for teaching listening comprehension. Unpublished manuscript.

Rivers, W. (Ed.). 1987. *Interactive Language Teaching*. Cambridge: Cambridge University Press.

Rivers, W., and M. Temperley. 1978. *A Practical Guide to the Teaching of English as a Second or Foreign Language*. New York: Oxford University Press.

Rutherford, W. 1987. *Second Language Grammar: Learning and Teaching*. London: Longman.

Smith, F. 1978. *Reading*. Cambridge: Cambridge University Press.

Sommers, N. 1980. Revision strategies of student writers and experienced adult writers. *College Composition and Communication*, 31, 4.

Stanovich, K. 1980. Toward an interactive-compensatory model of individual differences in the development of reading fluency. *Reading Research Quarterly*, 16, 32–71.

Varonis, E., and S. Gass. 1983. Target language input from non-native speakers. Paper presented at the Seventeenth Annual TESOL Convention, Toronto.

Wells, G. 1981. *Learning Through Interaction*. Cambridge: Cambridge University Press.

White, R. 1981. Approaches to writing. *Guidelines*, 6, 1–11.

Widdowson, H. 1987. Aspects of syllabus design. In M. Tickoo (Ed.) *Language Syllabuses: State of the Art*. Singapore: RELC.

Zamel, V. 1982. Writing: The process of discovering meaning. *TESOL Quarterly*, 16 (2), 495–9.

3 Task components

3.1 Introduction: identifying task components

The definition of a language learning task requires specification of four components: the goals, the input (linguistic or otherwise), the activities derived from this input, and finally the roles implied for teacher and learners. The question of roles will be addressed in the following chapter. This chapter looks in turn at the first three components in order to assist you in selecting, adapting, modifying and creating your own tasks.

There have been alternative breakdowns of the components of the task, from which I select three to draw on for my own analysis.

Candlin (1987) suggests that tasks should contain input, roles, settings, actions, monitoring, outcomes and feedback. Input refers to the data presented for learners to work on. Roles specify the relationship between participants in a task. Setting refers to the classroom and out-of-class arrangements entailed in the task. Actions are the procedures and sub-tasks to be performed by the learners. Monitoring refers to the supervision of the task in progress. Outcomes are the goals of the task, and feedback refers to the evaluation of the task.

Shavelson and Stern (1981), who are concerned with general educational planning rather than TESOL planning in particular, suggest that task design should take into consideration the following elements:

- content – the subject matter to be taught
- materials – the things that learners can observe/manipulate
- activities – the things the learners and teacher will be doing during the lesson
- goals – the teachers' general aim for the task (these are much more general and vague than objectives)
- students – their abilities, needs and interests are important
- social community – the class as a whole and its sense of 'groupness'

(Shavelson and Stern 1981: 478)

Wright (1987) suggests that tasks need minimally contain just two elements. These are input data which may be provided by materials, teachers or learners and an initiating question which instructs learners on what to do with the data. He rejects the notion that objectives or outcomes are obligatory on the grounds that, with certain tasks, a variety of outcomes might be possible and that these might be quite different from the ones anticipated by the teacher.

Wright's point concerning the unpredictability of outcomes is well made, and we shall bear in mind this necessary lack of definition in tasks, particularly when we consider the role of the learner in task planning and implementation. We shall likewise not lose sight of the influence of settings, including social community, and the necessity for feedback. Nevertheless, the framework which combines simplicity with the power to analyse the majority of learning tasks has just three components: goals, input and activities. These three in turn imply certain roles. The diagrammatic representation of the task and its constellation of elements is repeated here from Chapter 1.

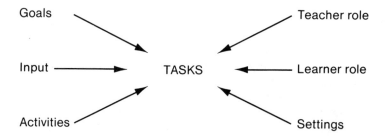

A framework for analysing communicative tasks

3.2 Goals

Defining and describing goals

Goals are the vague general intentions behind any given learning task. They provide a point of contact between the task and the broader curriculum. The answer that a teacher might give to the question: 'Why did you get learners to engage in Task X?' will generally take the form of some sort of goal statement. Possible answers might be:

'I wanted to develop their confidence in speaking.'
'I wanted to develop their personal writing skills.'
'I wanted to encourage them to negotiate information between each other to develop their interactional skills.'
'I wanted to develop their study skills.'

Goals may relate to a range of general outcomes (communicative, affective or cognitive) or may directly describe teacher or learner behaviour.

Another point worth noting is that goals are not always explicitly stated, although they can usually be inferred from an examination of a task. In addition there is rarely a simple one-to-one relationship between goals and tasks. In some cases a complex task involving a range of activities might be simultaneously moving learners towards several goals.

One classification of goals comes from a recent large-scale language curriculum project in Australia (the Australian Language Levels, or ALL, Project):

Goal Type	Example
Communicative	– establish and maintain interpersonal relations, and through this to exchange information, ideas, opinions, attitudes, and feelings, and to get things done
Socio-cultural	– have some understanding of the everyday life patterns of their contemporary age group in the target language speech community. This will cover their life at home, at school and at leisure
Learning-how-to-learn	– to negotiate and plan their work over a certain time span, and learn how to set themselves realistic objectives and how to devise the means to attain them
Language and cultural awareness	– to have some understanding of the systematic nature of language and the way it works

(Adapted from Clark 1987:227–32)

> How comprehensive are these goals? To what extent do they coincide with the sorts of goals which are either explicitly stated or implied in your own syllabus(es)?

Note that the goals are not necessarily mutually exclusive, and that there may be tasks which cover more than one goal. For example, a small group discussion on a socio-cultural theme might relate to both communicative and socio-cultural goals.

Task components

Since we are particularly concerned with communicative outcomes, it is worth noting that the ALL Project subcategorises communicative goals into three goal areas:

1. Establishing and maintaining interpersonal relationships, and through this to exchange information, ideas, opinions, attitudes and feelings, and to get things done.
2. Acquiring information from more or less 'public' sources in the target language (e.g. books, magazines, newspapers, brochures, documents, signs, notices, films, television, slides, tape, radio, public announcements, lectures or written reports etc.) and using this information in some way.
3. Listening to, reading, enjoying and responding to creative and imaginative uses of the target language (e.g. stories, poems, songs, rhymes, drama) and, for certain learners, creating them themselves.

(Adapted from Clark 1987: 226)

> How comprehensive are these goal areas? Can you think of any communicative tasks which do not fit into any of these categories?

Specialised and general purpose goals

In Chapter 2, we looked at the nature of language from a macroskill perspective, and looked at some of the skills which contribute to the mastery of a second language. This information can be drawn on in devising learning goals. For example, we saw that a broad distinction can be drawn between general 'everyday' English and English for specific purposes. In a similar way, we can distinguish between goals and teaching programmes which are aimed at teaching general 'everyday' English, and those whose purpose is to develop skills in specific specialised areas such as English for science and technology or English for tertiary study. Different purposes will be reflected in programme goals.

The broad distinction between general and specific outcomes can be applied to all four macroskill areas. As we saw in Chapter 2, a reading programme can be designed to provide learners with skills to carry out the hundred and one reading tasks that occur in daily life; from looking up a programme in the T.V. guide, to reading the sporting page of the afternoon newspaper. On the other hand, it might be designed to develop the specialised reading skills needed for studying successfully in a second language. Given the importance throughout the world of English as a medium of instruction at the tertiary level, it is not surprising that a great deal has been written about this second, specialised reading goal. Courses or modules for developing listening skills can also be divided into those focusing on general listening (for example understanding spoken media) and those for specialised listening (understanding university lectures).

Writing courses can be similarly divided into those which relate to basic functional language skills and those concerned with the development of more formal writing skills. Basic functional writing skills will include such things as writing notes to one's teacher, writing shopping lists, completing postcards and so on. Formal writing skills will include essay and report writing, writing business letters, and note taking from lectures and books.

Are the language programmes you are involved with directed primarily towards the development of general, everyday language skills, specialised language skills or both?
What might be the goal(s) of the following task? What particular skills is the task trying to develop?

>>>→

Activities

You are going away for a skiing holiday for ten days during the next month. You want someone to do *five* of the things below some time during that month. Choose the things you want people to do, and write them in the table below. For each one write the exact date(s) and a reason.

lend you their car	look after your cat while you're away
give you a lift to the airport	water your flowers while you're away
lend you their ski-boots	lend you £100
lend you a top hat	look after your children for a day
lend you their house for a week	help you decorate your living room for four days

I'm going to be on holiday from .... to .... (inclusive)

	I want someone to:	*Exact date(s)*	*Reason*
1			
2			
3			
4			
5			

Ask other people to help you with the five things, and explain why you want them to help. They will ask you to do things too: when you agree to do something, write it in the table below.

I have agreed to:	*Who for?*	*Exact date(s)*

Doff, Jones and Mitchell: Meanings into Words Intermediate, p. 57

3.3 Input

Input refers to the data that form the point of departure for the task. In fact, input for communicative tasks can be derived from a wide range of sources. Hover (1986) suggests the following:

– letters (formal/informal)	– calorie counter
– newspaper extracts	– recipe
– picture stories	– extract from a play
– Telecom account	– weather forecast
– driver's licence	– diary
– missing person's declaration form	– bus timetable
– social security form	– notice board items
– business cards	– housing request form
– memo note	– star signs
– photographs	– hotel entertainment programme
– family tree	– tennis court booking sheet
– drawings	– extracts from film script
– shopping lists	– high school year book
– invoices	– note to a friend
– postcards	– seminar programme
– hotel brochures	– newspaper reporter's notes
– passport photos	– UK travel regulations
– swop shop cards	– curriculum vitae
– street map	– economic graphs
– menu	
– magazine quiz	

This list, which is by no means exhaustive, illustrates the range of data sources which exist all around us. Most, with a little imagination, can form the basis for communicative tasks of one sort or another.

A similar range of stimulating source materials provides useful input for tasks which focus on writing. Morris and Stewart-Dore suggest that while it is probably neither necessary nor desirable for teachers to provide students with the opportunity of learning all the different styles and registers of writing, it is possible to extend the writing options traditionally offered to students by making the following forms available as examples:

- Articles for newspapers, magazines and journals.
- Reports to different kinds of groups.
- Radio and television scripts and documentaries.
- Puppet plays.
- News stories and reports.
- Research reports.
- Short stories, poems and plays.

Task components

— Press releases.
— Bulletins and newsletters.
— Editorials.
— Progress reports and plans for future development.
— Publicity brochures and posters.
— Instructions and handbooks.
— Recipes.
— Minutes of meetings.
— Scripts of group negotiations.
— Replies to letters and other forms of correspondence.
— Slide/tape presentations.
— Caption books to accompany a visual record of an experience.
— Comic strips for entertainment and information sharing.

(Morris and Stewart-Dore 1984: 158)

Make a list of the types of data which you use in your own classroom. Does the list include authentic material? Are learners exposed to a wide variety of data, or is your selection rather restricted?

The inclusion of such materials as input raises again the question of authenticity: what mixture of authentic and specially written material is valid? What do we mean by authenticity? A rule-of-thumb definition for 'authentic' here is any material which has not been specifically produced for the purposes of language teaching.

The argument for using authentic materials is derived from the notion, discussed in Chapter 2, that the most effective way to develop a particular skill is to rehearse that skill in class. Proponents of authentic materials point out that classroom texts and dialogues do not adequately prepare learners for coping with the language they hear and read in the real world outside the classroom. They argue that if we want learners to comprehend aural and written texts in the real world, then the learners need opportunities for engaging in these real-world texts in class. In relation to spoken language, Porter and Roberts (1981) suggest that materials written specifically for English language teaching have the following features which make them different from genuine speech.

Intonation
— marked by unusually wide and frequent pitch movement
Received pronunciation
— most speakers on British ELT tapes have an RP accent which is different from that which learners will normally hear in Britain
Enunciation
— words are enunciated with excessive precision

Structural repetition
– particular structures/functions recur with obtrusive frequency
Complete sentences
– sentences are short and well-formed
Distinct turn-taking
– one speaker waits until the other has finished
Pace
– this is typically slow
Quantity
– speakers generally say about the same amount
Attention signals
– these 'uhuh's' and 'mm's' are generally missing
Formality
– materials are biased toward standardised language; swearing and slang are rare
Limited vocabulary
– few references to specific, real-world entities and events
Too much information
– generally more explicit reference to people, objects and experiences than in real language
Mutilation
– texts rarely marred by outside noise

(Porter and Roberts 1981)

The following extracts have been taken from published course materials. The first has been specially written for ELT, while the second is an authentic conversation. Compare each with the above list to determine the extent to which Porter and Roberts have correctly identified the differences between authentic and non-authentic texts. Are there additional features which they have failed to identify? (You will, of course, not be able to make judgements about features such as pronunciation, enunciation and pace, as these would require you to hear the texts.)

》》》→

LET'S GO OUT!

1. Tom, Kate, Jeff, Anna are sitting around the table.

2.	Tom:	It's only 7 o'clock. Let's go out.
3.	Kate:	O.K. Where shall we go?
4.	Jeff:	I'd like a beer.
5.	Tom:	That's a good idea.
6.	Kate:	Oh no! I hate going to the pub. It's so boring . . .
7.		There's a good film on in the city.
8.	Tom:	No! I don't want to go to the movies.
9.	Kate:	Well I do. What about you, Anna?
10.	Anna:	I don't mind. You decide.
11.	Jeff:	I think it's too late to go to the city.
	Tom:	So do I!
12.	Kate:	It's *not* too late. We can hurry.
13.	Tom:	I don't agree with you. It *is* too late.
14.		Anyway there's a band playing at the pub tonight.
15.	Jeff:	Oh great! Let's go.
16.	Kate:	Oh no. It's so noisy at the pub.
17.		I want to go to the movies.
18.	Jeff:	Well, I'd rather go to the pub.
	Tom:	So would I.
19.	Kate:	O.K. You two can go to the pub and Anna and I will go to the movies.
20.	Anna:	Good idea, Kate, but hurry up.
21.	Kate:	I'm ready . . . Bye, boys, see you later!
22.	Tom/Jeff:	Oh, hang on a minute, wait a minute, we're coming.

Clemens and Crawford: Lifelines, p. 133

5c Me Tarzan

Authentic
Transcript

A	Marina calls Jane downstairs 'me Tarzan'	1
A&C	(laugh)	2
B	who? ·· Jane?	3
C	you know Jane?	4
B	no : ⌈which Jane?	5
C	⌊the lovely old woman	6
A	oh she's mad	7
C	with the glasses : she's lovely	8
A	and she dyes her hair	9
C	and she	10
B	what ⌈Jane?	11
C	⌊sits · you know where the	12
	switchboard's there · I'm si : I sit like that	13
	and the switchboard's there and she sits on	14
	the desk	15
A	oh you can't miss her she walks round	16
	going (gesture)	17

C	she's always there in the mor ·· oh she's	18
	nice : I like Jane she always takes your	19
	calls we have our little ⌈jokes	20
A	⌊mm she : she is nice	21
B	oh is she that ⌈old lady?	22
A	⌊but she al : she goes	23
	(gesture)	24
C	yeah	25
B	with the hair net	26
C	yeah (gestures)	27
A	yes (laughs)	28
A&B	(laugh)	29
B	oh she doesn't : that's cruel	30
A	no : well she started it because M : Marina	31
	could never remember her name : kept	32
	saying 'oh look I can't remember' she went	33
	: you know : 'me Tarzan you Jane' (laugh)	34
	and so Marina always refers to her as 'me	35
	Tarzan'	36

Slade and Norris: Teaching Casual Conversation Part Two, p. 81

Task components

The arguments for using authentic written texts in the classroom are similar to those advanced for authentic aural texts. In relation to second (as opposed to foreign) language contexts, Brosnan *et al.* (1984: 2) point out that the texts that learners will need to read in real life are in the environment around them – at the bank, in the letterbox, on shop doors and windows, on labels, packets etc. They do not have to be created by the teacher. Given the richness and variety of these resources, it should not be beyond even the beginning teacher to select texts which are appropriate to the needs, interests and proficiency levels of their students.

Brosnan *et al.* offer the following justifications for the use of these real-world materials.

— The language is natural. By simplifying language or altering it for teaching purposes (limiting structures, controlling vocabulary, etc.) we risk making the reading task more difficult. We may, in fact, be removing clues to meaning.
— It offers students the chance to deal with small amounts of print which, at the same time, contain complete and meaningful messages.
— It provides students with the opportunity to make use of non-linguistic clues (layout, pictures, colours, symbols, the physical setting in which it occurs) and so more easily to arrive at meaning from the printed word.
— Adults need to be able to see the immediate relevance of what they do in the classroom to what they need to do outside it, and real-life reading matter treated realistically makes the connection obvious.

(Brosnan *et al.* 1984:2–3)

> Study the data which have been used in the unit 'The Housing Committee' in Appendix A. Are the data authentic, or do you think they have been written in a way which is intended to make them look authentic?

For those language programmes whose goals relate to the development of academic skills, or which are preparing learners for further study, it has been suggested that texts can be taken from subject areas in the school curriculum (Widdowson 1978) and activities adapted from relevant academic disciplines. For example, by reading science texts, learners will develop a feel for scientific discourse (i.e. the way explanations and arguments are presented by scientists working in the particular branch of the discipline in question).

Each area of specialization, Science, Geography, Home Economics, Physical Education, Music, Art and so on, has its own body of literature, which presents the content of that area in a language style of its own. Once we recognize that different bodies of knowledge have their own literature and language style, we can see that the learning implications extend beyond the school scene to the world of work and everyday life.

(Morris and Stewart-Dore 1984: 21)

> Can you envisage difficulties for the high school English language specialist or ESP teacher at university level who is asked to help second language learners read science and mathematics texts? What, in your opinion, can the English language specialist offer learners which the content specialist is unable to do?

3.4 Activities

Activities specify what learners will actually do with the input which forms the point of departure for the learning task. I want, before we move on to some specific examples of activity types, to propose three general ways of characterising activities; rehearsal for the real world; skills use; and fluency/accuracy.

Authenticity

In Chapter 2, I suggested that tasks could be analysed according to the extent to which they required learners to rehearse, in class, the sort of skilled behaviour they might be expected to display in genuine communicative interaction outside the classroom. Here are two arguments from either side of the real-world/pedagogic fence:

> Classroom activities should parallel the 'real world' as closely as possible. Since language is a tool of communication, methods and materials should concentrate on the message, not the medium. In addition, the purposes of reading should be the same in class as they are in real life: 1) to obtain a specific fact or piece of information (scanning) 2) to obtain the general idea of the author (skimming) 3) to obtain a comprehensive understanding of a reading, as in reading a textbook (thorough comprehension), or 4) to evaluate information in order to determine where it fits into one's own system of beliefs (critical reading). Our students should become as critical as we are of the purposes for reading, so that they will be able to determine the proper approaches to a reading task.

(Clarke and Silberstein 1977:51)

> ... what is wanted is a methodology which will ... provide for communicative competence by functional investment. [Such a methodology] would engage the learners in problem-solving tasks as purposeful activities but without the rehearsal requirement that they should be realistic or 'authentic' as natural social behaviour.
>
> (Widdowson 1987:71)

Study the various activities associated with the units entitled 'Plan the House' and 'Spatial relationships' which are included in Appendix A. To what extent are these real-world or pedagogic activities? What aspects of communicative language use do you think learners might practise in carrying out these activities?

Before we leave the issue of authenticity, we need to take account of what we might term activity authenticity (in contrast with authenticity of input which has already been considered). While there is general acknowledgement that authentic materials have a place in the classroom, the issue of activity authenticity is less widely recognised. Candlin and Edelhoff (1982) point out that the authenticity issue involves much more than simply selecting texts from outside the arena of language teaching, and that the processes to which the learner submits aural and written texts and the things he or she is required to do with the data should also be authentic. Porter and Roberts (1981) also point out that while it is possible to use authentic texts in non-authentic ways, this severely limits the potential of the materials as resources for language learning.

Certain activities might only remotely resemble the sorts of things learners are required to do in the real world. However, they would probably be justified on the grounds that, in carrying out the activities, learners are required to practise skills which will be useful in the real world. (In Chapter 2, we also saw that certain activities are believed to stimulate as yet little understood processes of acquisition. We shall look at an example of these activities later in the section.)

To what extent do you think that the authentic/non-authentic distinction mirrors that between real-world and pedagogic activities?

Skill getting and skill using

Following Rivers and Temperley (1978), a second way of characterising activities is according to whether they are basically concerned with skill getting and skill using. These relate to the traditional distinction between controlled practice activities, in which learners manipulate phonological and grammatical forms, and transfer activities, in which learners are meant to apply their newly acquired mastery of linguistic forms to the comprehension and production of communicative language. Their scheme is represented in the following diagram.

Processes involved in learning to communicate

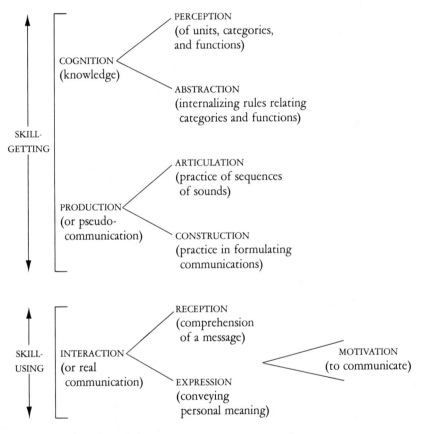

Rivers and Temperley: *A Practical Guide to the Teaching of English as a Second or Foreign Language*, p. 4

Does the skill-getting, skill-using distinction seem a useful one to you? Which are the more important in your classroom, skill-getting or skill-using activities? Study the following tasks. Are they designed for skill getting or skill using?

Task components

More exciting than knitting!!

I think sewing is far more difficult than knitting!

Well, I think it's much less difficult.

Anyhow, neither of them is as difficult as learning English!

Work in groups. Try to come to some sort of agreement between you on each of the activities in the list below. Decide which is the:

   most exciting   dullest   most dangerous   safest
   most energetic   most restful   most rewarding   most mindless

bufferfly collecting	cooking	disco dancing	sewing
learning a foreign language	cycling	hang-gliding	skiing
watching television	knitting	mountain climbing	parachuting
playing the piano	reading	playing football	fishing
stamp collecting	walking	scuba diving	swimming

It's the most ...

Joe's the tallest.
Pete's the youngest.
Jim's the most intelligent.
Ted's the oldest.

Work in groups. What can you say about *each one* of the items grouped together below, using *the most...* or *the -est...*?

apple grapefruit pineapple lemon	bicycle motorbike train camel	
Toronto Cambridge Athens Sao Paulo	wine beer brandy fruit juice	
January April July (in your country)	Rolls Royce Ferrari VW Beetle Land Rover	

It's much too big!

Work in small groups and write *four* sentences about each of the cartoons. For example:
   The van isn't big enough for the elephant to get in.
   The elephant's too big to get in the van.
   An elephant is such a big animal that it won't fit in a van.
   He's so big that we'll have to get a lorry.

Jones: Use of English, pp. 36–7

62

It is not always easy to decide whether a task is for 'skill getting' or 'skill using'. The tasks extracted from Jones, for instance, are designed to get students practising comparatives and superlatives and probably relate to Rivers and Temperley's level of 'pseudo-communication'. However, there is no reason why they might not also stimulate genuine communication. The extent to which tasks of various sorts do or do not promote genuine communication is something which, ultimately, can only be judged by observing the responses they actually promote in the classroom.

Accuracy and fluency

A third way of analysing learning activities is into those which focus the learner on developing accuracy, and those which focus on the development of fluency. Brumfit (1984) deals with the fluency/accuracy polarity in detail. He suggests that:

> . . . the demand to produce work for display to the teacher in order that evaluation and feedback could be supplied conflicted directly with the demand to perform adequately in the kind of natural circumstances for which teaching was presumably a preparation. Language display for evaluation tended to lead to a concern for accuracy, monitoring, reference rules, possibly explicit knowledge, problem solving and evidence of skill-getting. In contrast, language use requires fluency, expression rules, a reliance on implicit knowledge and automatic performance. It will on occasion also require monitoring and problem-solving strategies, but these will not be the most prominent features, as they tend to be in the conventional model where the student produces, the teacher corrects, and the student tries again.
>
> (Brumfit 1984: 51)

In his book, Brumfit makes the point that accuracy and fluency are not opposites, but are complementary: however materials and activities are often devised as if they were in conflict, and teachers certainly adjust their behaviour in the light of what is important to them at any particular point.

> You might like to examine your own teaching programme and decide on the extent to which learners are focused on fluency or accuracy.

The fluency/accuracy distinction is related to another dimension which can be used to analyse activities. This is the degree of teacher/learner control inherent in any activity. In classroom drills and other form-focused activities, control is usually very much with the teacher, while in simulations, role plays and the like, the learner has much more control. As power and control are aspects of teacher/learner roles, we shall defer further considerations of these to the next chapter.

Activity types

Let us now take a look at some activity types. The first has been noted in classroom-centred research directed towards the question: 'What classroom activities and patterns of organisation stimulate interactive language use?' It has been found that small-group, two-way information gap tasks seem to be particularly appropriate for stimulating such language. A two-way task is one in which each participant has some knowledge not shared by any other participant. The participants are then set a task or a problem which can only be solved if they pool their information. Doughty and Pica (1986), who have conducted some interesting experiments into the use of small-group information gaps, provide the following example of a two-way task. This is called the 'plant the garden' task.

For the task, one needs a felt board master 'garden', individual 'gardens' and a number of loose felt flowers which are to be 'planted'. An example is provided opposite.

As you can see, each of the participants' gardens contains part of the hidden master garden. Without looking at each other's boards, learners are required to communicate with each other and thereby replicate the hidden master garden.

Doughty and Pica's two-way task is one which learners are hardly likely to want to carry out in the real world. However, learners will get to rehearse skills such as mobilising grammatical knowledge, mastering pronunciation etc. which will help in genuine communicative interaction outside the classroom.

> Look through the materials in Appendix A and see whether you can find examples of one- and two-way tasks. Are there any activities which might be adapted or modified to turn them into one- and two-way tasks?

FIGURE 1

Required Information Exchange Task

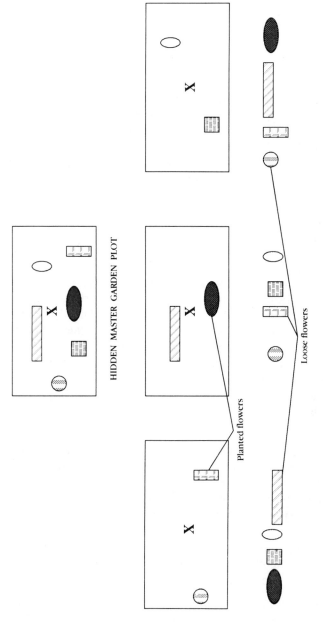

HIDDEN MASTER GARDEN PLOT

Planted flowers

Loose flowers

INDIVIDUAL PARTICIPANT BOARDS

Note: This is a reduced version, using abstract figures to represent the flowers used in the task.

Doughty and Pica (1986)

Task components

We shall now look at three different activity typologies, proposed by Prabhu, Clark and Pattison.

In the Bangalore Project, three principal activity types are used: information gap, reasoning gap, opinion gap. These are explained as follows:

1 *Information-gap activity,* which involves a transfer of given information from one person to another – or from one form to another, or from one place to another – generally calling for the decoding or encoding of information from or into language.[1] One example is pair work in which each member of the pair has a part of the total information (for example an incomplete picture) and attempts to convey it verbally to the other. Another example is completing a tabular representation with information available in a given piece of text. The activity often involves selection of relevant information as well, and learners may have to meet criteria of completeness and correctness in making the transfer.

2 *Reasoning-gap activity,* which involves deriving some new information from given information through processes of inference, deduction, practical reasoning, or a perception of relationships or patterns. One example is working out a teacher's timetable on the basis of given class timetables. Another is deciding what course of action is best (for example cheapest or quickest) for a given purpose and within given constraints. The activity necessarily involves comprehending and conveying information, as an information-gap activity, but the information to be conveyed is not identical with that initially comprehended. There is a piece of reasoning which connects the two.

3 *Opinion-gap activity,* which involves identifying and articulating a personal preference, feeling, or attitude in response to a given situation. One example is story completion; another is taking part in the discussion of a social issue. The activity may involve using factual information and formulating arguments to justify one's opinion, but there is no objective procedure for demonstrating outcomes as right or wrong, and no reason to expect the same outcome from different individuals or on different occasions.

Prabhu: Second Language Pedagogy, pp. 46–7

> Can you find examples of these activity types in
> Appendix A?

Clark (1987) proposes seven broad communicative activity types (these
are expansions of the three communicative goal types we looked at in
3.2). Language programmes, he suggests, should enable learners to:

- solve problems through social interaction with others, for
  example, participate in conversation related to the pursuit of a
  common activity with others, obtain goods and services and
  necessary information through conversation or correspondence,
  make arrangements and come to decisions with others
  (convergent tasks);
- establish and maintain relationships and discuss topics of
  interest through the exchange of information, ideas, opinions,
  attitudes, feelings, experiences and plans (divergent tasks);
- search for specific information for some given purpose, process
  it, and use it in some way (for example, find out the cheapest
  way to go from A to B);
- listen to or read information, process it, and use it in some way
  (for example, read a news item and discuss it with someone,
  read an article and summarize it, listen to a lecture and write
  notes on it);
- give information in spoken or written form on the basis of
  personal experience (for example, give a talk, write a report,
  write a diary, record a set of instructions on how to do
  something, or fill in a form);
- listen to, read or view a story, poem, feature etc. and perhaps
  respond to it personally in some way (for example, read a story
  and discuss it);
- create an imaginative text (for some learners only).

(Clark 1987: 238–9)

> All of these activity types could involve learners in oral
> interaction. Look through your own repertoire of
> activities for oral interaction (or examine a coursebook
> you have used or are thinking of using), and find
> examples of each of these activity types. Were there any
> activity types for which you could not find examples?

Task components

Pattison (1987) also proposes seven activity types. These are as follows:

1. *Questions and answers*
   These activities are based on the notion of creating an information gap by letting learners make a personal and secret choice from a list of language items which all fit into a given frame (e.g. the location of a person or object). The aim is for learners to discover their classmates' secret choices. This activity can be used to practise almost any structure, function or notion.

2. *Dialogues and role-plays*
   These can be wholly scripted or wholly improvised, however, 'If learners are given some choice of what to say, and if there is a clear aim to be achieved by what they say in their role-plays, they may participate more willingly and learn more thoroughly than when they are told to simply repeat a given dialogue in pairs'.

3. *Matching activities*
   Here, the task for the learner is to recognise matching items, or to complete pairs or sets. 'Bingo', 'Happy families' and 'Split dialogues' (where learners match given phrases) are examples of matching activities.

4. *Communication strategies*
   These are activities designed to encourage learners to practise communication strategies such as paraphrasing, borrowing or inventing words, using gesture, asking for feedback, simplifying.

5. *Pictures and picture stories*
   Many communication activities can be stimulated through the use of pictures (e.g. spot the difference, memory test, sequencing pictures to tell a story).

6. *Puzzles and problems*
   Once again, there are many different types of puzzles and problems. These require learners to 'make guesses, draw on their general knowledge and personal experience, use their imagination and test their powers of logical reasoning'.

7. *Discussions and decisions*
   These require the learner to collect and share information to reach a decision (e.g. to decide which items from a list are essential to have on a desert island).

The Clark and Pattison typologies are quite different. Clark focuses on the sorts of uses to which we put language in the real world, while Pattison has a much more pedagogic focus.

Consider again some of the activities in Appendix A. To what extent do these reflect the above activity typologies? Can the activities be assigned to one or more of the Clark and Pattison activity types or not?
You might, at this point, like to pause and consider the three typologies I have presented from Prabhu, Clark and Pattison.
Which activities from the three typologies do you prefer? What does this tell you about your own approach to and beliefs about language teaching?

We shall now look at some proposals relating the development of literacy skills.

In their work on reading in the content areas, Morris and Stewart-Dore develop a four-stage model which they use for categorising reading activities. This model is as follows.

Learning to Learn from Text

TEACHER CONCERN	ERICA* STAGE USED
1. Students have difficulty using the text effectively	PREPARING
2. Students can 'read' but do not understand what they read	THINKING THROUGH
3. Students copy rather than change ideas into their own words	EXTRACTING AND ORGANIZING INFORMATION
4. Students cannot summarize or express themselves clearly, and accurately in writing	TRANSLATING

Morris and Steward-Dore: Learning to Learn from Text, p. 46

What activities can you think of/identify in your course materials for each of the stages outlined in the model?

In preparing learners for a reading assignment, Morris and Stewart-Dore suggest the development of structured overviews. The two following

(*Effective Reading in the Content Areas*)

overviews have been developed from texts on 'family structures' and 'motor manufacturing'.

These overviews are designed to provide learners with the appropriate mental maps or 'schema' for encouraging them to relate their own background knowledge to text content. The structured overviews can be dealt with in a variety of ways. For example, learners in small groups

Structured Overview: Family Structures.

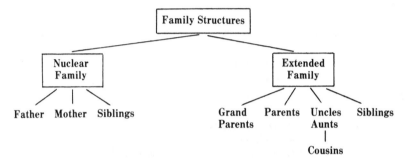

Structured Overview: Motor Manufacturing.

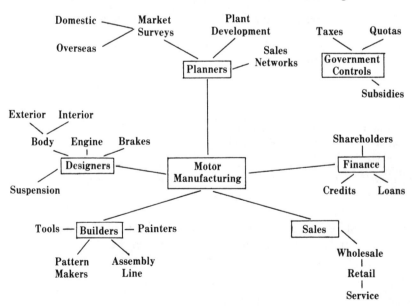

ibid, p. 50

could be given the outline in skeleton form with the words deleted and words presented on a separate list. Their task would be to insert the words in the appropriate place on the outline. Another, easier task, would be to put some of the words in the wrong place on the overview and ask learners to 'spot the mistakes'.

At the thinking-through stage, learners are confronted with activities designed to encourage them to process the text in some depth and to draw conclusions from the content. Suitable activities at this level include cloze exercises and 'three-level guides'. Three-level guides are designed to take readers through three stages of discourse processing. Stage 1 involves locating information (i.e. seeing what the writer actually says), Stage 2 involves interpreting what the author means, and Stage 3 involves using the information in some way.

The following example shows a text exploited at these three levels. Students complete the activities individually or in small groups, and then work in small groups to compare responses and develop a group consensus.

THE MACDONNELL RANGES

The MacDonnell Ranges in the Northern Territory of Australia are surrounded by a vast area of near desert lands. There are rugged mountain ranges running east-west with wide gently-sloped valleys between. North and south of the mountains are broad, undulating lands covered with spinifex and mulga.

The land here is constantly dry and hot. Rainfall is not reliable and there are frequent droughts when the blazing sun shines down day after day for years. When the rain does come, grasses and flowers spring to life and a new land is born.

People who live in this area raise cattle. Because of the harsh conditions, the number of cattle per square kilometre is very low and averages between one and five beasts. Imagine one cow needing anywhere between 60 and 320 hectares to feed itself. Obviously with such a low stocking-rate, properties have to be very large and are measured in tens and even hundreds of thousands of hectares.

In drought years, station owners suffer heavy losses. Water holes dry up and cattle die of starvation and thirst. Between 1960 and 1966, the number of cattle was halved in some areas. The station owners restock their properties in good years and try to rebuild their herds. Unfortunately, this takes time because the land also has to recover.

Level 1. Tick the statements which focus on what the author says in this summary. When you have made your decisions, discuss your choices and your reasons with your group.
- (a) The MacDonnell Ranges are rugged mountains.
- (b) The MacDonnell Ranges are in a very hot-dry area.
- (c) Droughts can last for a few days.
- (d) People who live here raise sheep.

Task components

    —(e) The harsh conditions keep the number of cattle down.
    —(f) Properties are very large.
    —(g) Cattle drink from water-holes.
    —(h) The land also has to recover.
    —(i) Station owners rebuild their herds in good years.

Level 2. Tick the statements which you think mean what the author meant in the summary. Discuss your choices with your group, and be prepared to justify them.

    —(a) The MacDonnell Ranges are very isolated, lonely places.
    —(b) Grasses and flowers seed themselves naturally.
    —(c) Grass and flower seeds are long lived.
    —(d) Cattle in the MacDonnell Range country are very hardy.
    —(e) People who live on properties in this area have no close neighbours.
    —(f) Raising cattle in the MacDonnell Ranges is not a very reliable business.
    —(g) The years 1960-1966 were drought years.
    —(h) A new land was born in the MacDonnell Ranges in 1967.

Level 3. Tick the statements which you think the author would support. Be ready to give your reasons when you discuss your choices.

    —(a) People have to learn to take the rough with the smooth.
    —(b) Cattle from the MacDonnell Ranges probably need fattening-up somewhere else before being sent to market.
    —(c) Children who live on large cattle properties probably get very little schooling.

ibid, pp. 101–2

At Stage 3, the extracting and organising information stage, learners are encouraged to discriminate the more important information in a text from the supporting detail and to organise this information in some way. This can be done by getting learners to transform information contained in a text into diagrams, charts, outlines, etc.

The final stage in the process involves translating information from reading to writing. This stage is essentially concerned with helping students develop skills in summarising and expressing themselves clearly and accurately in writing. Information obtained through reading can be conveyed through a range of activities, including prose summaries, note-form outlines, short and long answers to assignment questions, reports, letters, descriptions of process and methods and essays (Morris and Stewart-Dore 1984: 142). It is important for activities at this level to focus learners on doing something meaningful with the information they have extracted. Too often, the writing class becomes one in which learners simply copy sections of text.

Grellet (1981) provides the following typology for reading comprehension activities:

Reading techniques

I SENSITIZING
  1 Inference; through the context
    Inference: through
    word-formation
  2 Understanding relations within
    the sentence
  3 Linking sentences and ideas:
    reference
    Linking sentences and ideas:
    link-words

2 IMPROVING READING SPEED

3 FROM SKIMMING TO SCANNING
  1 Predicting
  2 Previewing
  3 Anticipation
  4 Skimming
  5 Scanning

How the aim is conveyed

I AIM AND FUNCTION OF THE TEXT
  1 Function of the text
  2 Functions within the text

2 ORGANIZATION OF THE TEXT:
DIFFERENT THEMATIC PATTERNS
  1 Main idea and supporting
    details
  2 Chronological sequence
  3 Descriptions
  4 Analogy and contrast
  5 Classification
  6 Argumentative and logical
    organization

3 THEMATIZATION

Understanding meaning

I NON–LINGUISTIC RESPONSE TO THE
TEXT
  1 Ordering a sequence of pictures
  2 Comparing texts and pictures
  3 Matching
  4 Using illustrations
  5 Completing a document
  6 Mapping it out
  7 Using the information in the text
  8 Jigsaw reading

2 LINGUISTIC RESPONSE TO THE TEXT
  1 Reorganizing the information:
    reordering events
    Reorganizing the information:
    using grids
  2 Comparing several texts
  3 Completing a document
  4 Question-types
  5 Study skills: summarizing
    Study skills: note-taking

Assessing the text

I FACT VERSUS OPINION

2 WRITER'S INTENTION

Grellet: Developing Reading Skills, pp. 12 and 13

Task components

Activities in the first section (Reading Techniques) are designed to develop basic reading skills and strategies. Sensitising activities are designed to help learners cope with unfamiliar words and grammatical structures. Learners are taught to infer the meaning of unknown elements, to understand relations within the sentence (in particular, to identify subject and verb), and to link sentences and ideas, particularly those which are signalled by cohesion. Learners are also encouraged to increase their reading speed, and to develop flexible reading strategies (in particular, scanning for specific information, and skimming for an overview of the text).

The second set of activities focus the learner on how writers convey their aim through the function and organisation of the text. Learners are taught to identify the function of the text by utilising linguistic and non-linguistic clues. They are also taught to identify the essential organisation of the text, whether it is through the expansion of a main idea, and/or whether it is organised in terms of chronological sequence, description, analogy and contrast, classification, argument and logic. Finally, learners are sensitised to the mechanics of thematisation. They are shown how altering the order of elements in a sentence can alter the meaning.

Activities which focus on meaning are designed to get learners to process the content of the text through the various types of non-linguistic and linguistic responses they might make to the text. The activities have two different aims:

1. To make students active in the reading process by presenting them with decision-making activities (e.g. drawing a diagram with the information given in the text, solving the problem, completing a table which reorganises the information).
2. To devise activities which are as natural as possible, i.e. as close as possible to what one would naturally do with the text (e.g. answering a letter using the information given in that letter, completing a document, comparing several texts etc.).

(Grellet 1981: 22)

The final set of activities is designed to get readers to go beneath the surface of the text, as it were, in order to judge it and evaluate it. Here readers are required to differentiate fact from opinion and to identify the writer's attitudes, intentions and biases.

> What are the similarities and differences between the activity types of Grellet, and those of Morris and Stewart-Dore? Which scheme is closest to your own approach to the teaching of reading?

Both typologies analyse the reading process in terms of the cognitive demands made on the reader. The scheme presented by Morris and Stewart-Dore moves from extracting information, through understanding text structure, to going beyond the text and transforming and restructuring text content in some way.

Grellet's typology is more comprehensive, although somewhat less coherent. Some of the elements relate to reading techniques (for example skimming and scanning), some to rhetorical functions (chronological sequence, classification), some to cognitive operations (understanding relations within the sentence) and yet others to classroom tasks (jigsaw reading, reorganising information using grids).

Appendix C presents sets of activities graded at seven levels of difficulty. These lists are more explicit and detailed than either of the Morris and Stewart-Dore or Grellet typologies. The reading tasks are graded in terms of a) the size and complexity of the text confronting the reader and b) what the learner is required to do with the text. (Issues relating to task difficulty and grading are taken up in Chapter 5.)

In the remainder of this section, we shall look at some proposals for teaching writing. We saw in Chapter 2 that, in the development of writing skills, there has been a debate over whether activities should focus learners on the process of composing, or on developing mastery of the mechanics of writing.

> Does the following quote advocate activities which focus on product or process?

> There are a number of advantages to asking students to begin writing with whole words, particularly personal information or their own oral language. We are encouraging them to see letters as being grouped into meaningful units, rather than as isolated sounds. However, this focus on a global approach can produce problems if students consistently have problems in accurately reproducing the letter shapes. It may be necessary to backtrack occasionally, to demonstrate letter formation or the placement of letters on a line. We may find for example that having been given a typed copy of a language experience story to copy, students are too faithfully reproducing the typewriter's letter shapes; or that the lack of lines on the typed sheet has not given them sufficient guidance as to where the letters they write should sit in relation to the lines on the page. We would then have to go back to some of these pre-writing activities that provide help with these specific problems.
>
> (Bell and Burnaby 1984: 68)

Task components

The pre-writing activities mentioned by Bell and Burnaby are designed to give learners control over the mechanics of the language. While such activities may be considered necessary for learners whose first language does not use the Roman alphabet, the activities themselves can be boring, particularly for adolescents and adults. Are there then ways of avoiding activities involving mere copying and mechanical reproduction, even with low level learners?

> The tasks in the table which follow have been extracted from a recent book on writing. Which of these tasks are familiar to you, and which are new?
> Can you relate them to the activity typologies already presented?
> Are the tasks basically real-world or pedagogic ones?

TABLE I.   A SELECTION OF WRITING TASKS

Data	Activity
1. A set of model sentences and a list of unpunctuated sentences.	Note the use of capital letters in the model sentences and then indicate where capitals are needed in the unpunctuated list.
2. A letter in which the sentences are scrambled.	Study the letter and rearrange the sentences so they are in the correct order.
3. A letter and a conversation.	Read the letter and write a similar one based on the information in the dialogue.
4. Two versions of a particular story.	Study the two versions, decide which you like best and why. Write a story based on the one you prefer.
5. A set of photographs.	Choose at least six of the photographs and arrange them in an order which makes a good story. Discuss and then write the story.
6. A paragraph with the first and last sentences missing. Sets of possible first and last sentences.	Select the most appropriate first and last sentences from the alternatives provided.

(Adapted from Coe, Rycroft and Ernest 1983)

3.5 Conclusion

In this chapter, we have looked at task goals, input and activities. The discussion and examples have demonstrated two difficulties: the difficulty of separating syllabus from methodology; and the difficulty of isolating individual skills when fully communicative behaviour is being encouraged.

At the same time, we have developed a system for describing learning tasks which can accommodate a wide range of teaching and learning behaviour from the conventional to the 'experimental'. We have looked in detail at the arguments surrounding the use of authentic material to elicit authentic responses, and have seen how the real-world/pedagogic distinction manifests itself in all the task components. We have also touched on the question of learner independence and the unpredictability of outcome in tasks where the interpretation and intention of the learner may differ from that of the teacher.

In the next chapter we shall look in greater detail at the roles of teacher and learner as they are implied in different kinds of task.

References and further reading

Bell, J. and B. Burnaby. 1984. *A Handbook for ESL Literacy*. Toronto: OISE.

Brosnan, D., K. Brown, and S. Hood. 1984. *Reading in Context*. Adelaide: National Curriculim Resource Centre.

Brumfit, C. 1984. *Communicative Methodology in Language Teaching*. Cambridge: Cambridge University Press.

Candlin, C. 1987. Towards task-based language learning. In Candlin and Murphy (Eds.).

Candlin, C., and C. Edelhoff. 1982. *Challenges: Teacher's Book*. London: Longman.

Candlin, C. and D. Murphy (Eds.). 1987. *Language Learning Tasks*. Englewood Cliffs NJ: Prentice-Hall.

Clark, J. 1987. *Curriculum Renewal in School Foreign Language Learning*. Oxford: Oxford University Press.

Clarke, M., and S. Silberstein. 1977. Toward a realization of psycholinguistic principles in the ESL reading class. *Language Learning*, 27 (1), 48–65.

Clemens, J., and J. Crawford. 1986. *Lifelines*. Adelaide: National Curriculum Resource Centre.

Coe, N., R. Rycroft, and P. Ernest. 1983. *Writing Skills: A Problem-Solving Approach*. Cambridge: Cambridge University Press.

Doff, A., C. Jones, and K. Mitchell. 1983. *Meaning into Words: Intermediate*. Cambridge: Cambridge University Press.

Doughty, C., and T. Pica. 1986. 'Information gap' tasks: Do they facilitate second language acquisition? *TESOL Quarterly*, 20 (2), 305–25.

Grellet, F. 1981. *Developing Reading Skills*. Cambridge: Cambridge University Press.

Hover, D. 1986. *Think Twice*. Cambridge: Cambridge University Press.

Jones, L. 1984. *Ideas*. Cambridge: Cambridge University Press.

Jones, L. 1985. *Use of English*. Cambridge: Cambridge University Press

Morris, A., and N. Stewart-Dore. 1984. *Learning to Learn from Text: Effective Reading in the Content Areas*. Sydney: Addison-Wesley.

Pattison, P. 1987. *Developing Communication Skills*. Cambridge: Cambridge University Press.

Porter, D., and J. Roberts. 1981. Authentic listening activities. *English Language Teaching Journal*, 36 (1), 37–47.

Prabhu, N. 1987. *Second Language Pedagogy: A Perspective*. Oxford: Oxford University Press.

Rivers, W., and M. Temperley. 1978. *A Practical Guide to the Teaching of English as a Second or Foreign Language*. New York: Oxford University Press.

Shavelson, R., and P. Stern. 1981. Research on teachers' pedagogical thoughts, judgements, decisions and behaviour. *Review of Educational Research*, 51 (4), 455–98.

Slade, D., and L. Norris. 1986. *Teaching Casual Conversation*. Adelaide: National Curriculum Resource Centre.

Widdowson, H. 1978. *Teaching Language as Communication*. Oxford: Oxford University Press.

Widdowson, H. 1987. Aspects of syllabus design. In M. Tickoo (Ed.). *Language Syllabuses: State of the Art*. Singapore: RELC.

Wright, T. 1987. Instructional task and discoursal outcome in the L2 classroom. In Candlin and Murphy (Eds.).

4 Roles and settings in the language class

4.1 Introduction

In this chapter we shall look at the roles of teachers and learners which are implicit in learning tasks, and also at the settings in which learning takes place. I have included these as a separate chapter because of the importance they assume from the perspective of communicative language teaching and also because, as they are usually implicit, roles and settings are different in type from goals, input and activities.

We shall look first at the different learner roles which are implied by different methodological approaches, and by tasks which focus learners on language and learning rather than on meaning. We shall then look at the complementary roles of teachers, and at the close relationship between learner and teacher roles.

We shall then look at an aspect of teaching which is closely related to roles. This is the setting in which tasks take place.

4.2 Learner roles

'Role' refers to the part that learners and teachers are expected to play in carrying out learning tasks as well as the social and interpersonal relationships between the participants. In their comprehensive analysis of approaches and methods in language teaching, Richards and Rodgers (1986) devote considerable attention to learner and teacher roles. They point out that a method (and, in our case, a task) will reflect assumptions about the contributions that learners can make to the learning process. The following table is based on the analysis carried out by Richards and Rodgers. (Appendix B gives further details, although it is not a part of the aim of this book to describe fully the approaches and methods outlined in the table on page 80.)

≫→

Roles and settings

Approach	Roles
1. Oral/Situational	– learner listens to teacher and repeats; no control over content or methods
2. Audiolingual	– learner has little control; reacts to teacher direction; passive, reactive role
3. Communicative	– learner has an active, negotiative role; should contribute as well as receive
4. Total Physical Response	– learner is a listener and performer; little influence over content and none over methodology
5. The Silent Way	– learners learn through systematic analysis; must become independent and autonomous
6. Community Language Learning	– learners are members of a social group or community; move from dependence to autonomy as learning progresses
7. The Natural Approach	– learners play an active role and have relatively high degree of control over content language production
8. Suggestopedia	– learners are passive, have little control over content or methods

This analysis demonstrates the wide variety of learner roles which are possible in the language class. These include the following:

– the learner is the passive recipient of outside stimuli;
– the learner is an interactor and negotiator who is capable of giving as well as taking;
– the learner is a listener and performer who has little control over the content of learning;
– the learner is involved in a process of personal growth;
– the learner is involved in a social activity, and the social and inter-personal roles of the learner cannot be divorced from psychological learning processes;
– learners must take responsibility for their own learning, developing autonomy and skills in learning-how-to-learn.

The last point raises the important issue of learners developing an awareness of themselves as learners. There is some controversy about whether or not learners should consciously reflect on language structure and learning processes, although there seems to be a growing consensus that such reflection is valuable. There is also evidence that different learners will benefit from different learning strategies, and that they should therefore be encouraged to find out and apply those strategies which suit them best (Willing 1988). The range of strategies can be seen in the following list from Rubin and Thompson 1982 (the glosses following each strategy are from Candlin and Nunan 1987). The strategies have been reproduced here, because they require learners to adopt a range of roles which are relatively uncommon in traditional instruction. They require the learner to be adaptable, creative, inventive, and most of all independent.

1. *Finding your own way*
   Helping learners to discover what ways of learning work best for them. For example, how they best learn vocabulary items. It also implies learners discovering other ways of learning from other learners in the class, and using all senses to learn in as independent a way as they can.
2. *Organising information about language*
   Developing ways for learners to organise what they have learned, through making notes and charts, grouping items and displaying them for easy reference.
3. *Being creative*
   Experimenting with different ways of creating and using language, for example with new ways of using words, playing with different arrangements of sounds and structures, inventing imaginative texts and playing language games.
4. *Making your own opportunities*
   Learning language actively by performing tasks in class, for example by interacting with fellow learners and the teacher, asking questions, listening regularly to the language, reading different kinds of texts and practising writing. There is much scope for rehearsal in the language class.
5. *Learning to live with uncertainty*
   Not always relying on certain and safe answers but trying to work things out with the help of resources, for example using dictionaries. We might include here helping learners to keep on talking and to understand the general gist of texts, rather than every language item in them.
6. *Using mnemonics*
   Helping learners find quick ways of recalling what they have learned, for example through rhymes, word associations, word classes, particular contexts of occurrence, experiences and personal memories.

7. *Making errors work*
   Learning to live with errors and helping learners to prevent errors from blocking their participation in tasks. Helping learners to ask for error correction and help and to learn from the errors they will make. It helps if learners can estimate the relative gravity of errors and realise that errors vary according to channel and text-type.

8. *Using your linguistic knowledge*
   Helping learners make comparisons with what they know about language from their own mother tongue, as well as building on what they have already learned in the new language, both in terms of formal rules and conventions for language use.

9. *Letting the context help you*
   Help learners to realise the relationships that exist between words, sounds, and structures, developing their capacity to guess and infer meanings from the surrounding context and from their background knowledge and out-of-class experience.

10. *Learning to make intelligent guesses*
    Developing the learners' capacity to work out meanings. Specifically, to focus both on the main parts of the message and to relate these to the overall text and context. To guess on the basis of probabilities of occurrence and meaning, and to try to work from what is relevant to the text and task in hand.

11. *Learning formalised routines*
    Encouraging learners to learn routines and whole phrases. Idioms, routinised expressions, sound sequences, dialogue extracts, are all examples of this, as are ways of expressing a variety of interpersonal functions.

12. *Learning production techniques*
    Helping learners not to be so much concerned with accuracy that they do not develop the capacity to be fluent. In particular, to develop their paraphrasing ability, their willingness to ask for help and their use of gestures and other devices to keep on talking.

13. *Using different styles of speech and writing*
    Developing learners' ability to differentiate between styles of speech and writing, both productively and 'receptively'. Finding ways to transfer their mother tongue experience of such variation to the new language.

> To what extent do your own teaching tasks and materials encourage learners to explore and apply strategies such as these?

While learning strategies, learning-how-to-learn tasks and grammatical awareness tasks, which invite learners to reflect on language and learning, might appear to be non-communicative, they can, as Comeau (1987) points out, be devised in ways which make them interactive and communicative. Rutherford (1987) also provides many examples of grammatical consciousness-raising activities which can stimulate genuine communication between learners.

Any activities which encourage learners to think about the nature of language and ways of learning imply a more critical and reflective learner role than those in which the learner is memorising or manipulating language. They are now operating at a meta-linguistic level.

Activities to encourage such reflection can be found in any of the skills areas. In the area of spelling, for instance, Bell and Burnaby make the following suggestions:

> a) trying to decide from its sound which letter a word begins with, and at least trying to get that down:
> b) putting down any other letters which they know they can hear the sound of;
> c) breaking the word into syllables for possible clues;
> d) thinking of rhyming words that they know how to spell (e.g. attack 'now' by analogy with 'how'), or which begin in the same way (e.g. attempt 'real' by comparison with 'read');
> e) reading back what they have so far, to see what it sounds like;
> f) asking somebody for help;
> g) using a dictionary.
>
> (Bell and Burnaby 1984: 75)

These activities are designed to encourage a reflective attitude on the part of the learner.

One role receiving increasing attention is that of the student as independent learner. Dickinson (1987) argues strongly for the use of self-instruction and the development of independent learning skills on the following grounds:

1. *Practical reasons*
   In some situations, it is impossible for learners to attend regular classes. For these learners, it is a matter of self-instruction or nothing.
2. *Individual differences*
   Self-instruction enables us to cope with differences in aptitude, cognitive styles and strategies, and learning strategies.
3. *Educational aims*
   Self-instruction facilitates the development of strategies which seem to characterise the 'good' language learner. It also promotes autonomy and fulfils requirements for continuing education.
4. *Motivation*
   Self-instruction can have a positive effect on motivation.
5. *Learning how to learn*
   This reason cuts across several of the others already summarised.

Finding out about learning processes, planning learning and then using appropriate and preferred strategies is a basic and important educational objective.

4.3 Teacher roles

Turning from a focus on the roles of learners to those of the teacher, Richards and Rodgers (1986) suggest that learner roles are closely related to the functions and status of the teacher. They point out that some methods are totally teacher dependent, while others view the teacher as a catalyst, consultant or guide. Some years ago, there was even an attempt to 'teacher-proof' instruction by limiting the role of the teacher to that of 'manager of materials'.

Richards and Rodgers point out that teacher roles are related to the following issues:

- the types of functions teachers are expected to fulfil, e.g. whether that of practice director, counselor or model
- the degree of control the teacher has over how learning takes place
- the degree to which the teacher is responsible for content
- the interactional patterns that develop between teachers and learners

(Richards and Rodgers 1986: 24)

> What assumptions do you or your teaching organisation hold about the roles of teachers and learners? Do you think there is any need for these views to be modified or adapted?

Problems are likely to occur when there is a mismatch between the role perceptions of the teacher and the learner. For example, it is not uncommon in adult ESL classes for the teacher to see herself as a guide and catalyst for classroom communication while the learners see her as someone who should be providing explicit instruction and modelling the target language. In such situations, it is necessary for there to be consultation and negotiation between teachers and learners.

Dubin and Olshtain (1986) look at a range of metaphors for providing an account of teacher and learner roles. They suggest that:

> The terms *play* and *players* hold out a rich potential for developing a metaphor concerning language learners. Only superficially is play a recreational activity, confined to the interests of children. . . . As

a player, one must participate actively. At the same time, one must concentrate by observing what others do. Players take part in all of the interactional configurations which are important in a communicative language course: as individuals, in pairs, in small groups, and in whole group displays. As players, participants can come to view language learning as something quite different from 'knowing' which they associate with other schooling experiences in their lives.

(Dubin and Olshtain 1986: 81–2)

One might think that in reading and writing tasks, being essentially solitary activities, learners will adopt a restricted range of roles. In fact, the roles can be as varied and diverse as they are in oral/aural language work.

> What role for the teacher is implicit in the following statement? Do you think this is a reasonable attitude to take, or is it extreme?

The teacher as teacher is necessary only when the class is attempting to resolve a language problem, for it is only in this situation that the teacher is automatically presumed to possess more knowledge than the students. This role can be minimized if the students' attack strategies and reading skills have been effectively developed. If the task is realistic, and if the students have learned to adjust their reading strategies according to the task, there should be little need for teacher intervention.

(Clarke and Silberstein 1977:52)

Traditionally, the role of the teacher in the writing class is to provide correct models to set tasks and to provide corrective feedback. The role of the learner is the rather passive one of coming up with the correct target language forms.

> In what ways are the roles of teachers and learners in the following different from these as 'traditionally' conceived?

Writing taught as a process of discovery implies that revision becomes the main focus of the course and that the teacher, who traditionally provides feedback after the fact, intervenes to guide students through the process. Teacher-student conferences need to be regularly held between drafts so that students can learn, while they are creating, what areas need to be worked on. Some educators feel that individual conferences are so effective that they should take the place of in-class instruction (Carnicelli, 1980). This, however, would deny the students the opportunity to share their writing with other students, an activity that forms the basis of much process-centred instruction . . . This shared experience reinforces the fact that the teacher is truly not the only reader . . . Moreover, this type of experience helps develop in students the crucial ability of reviewing their writing with the eyes of another.

(Zamel 1982:47)

Power and control

In Chapter 2, brief mention was made of the fact that tasks can be analysed in terms of power and control. Drills and the like vest power in the teacher, while communicative tasks such as role plays, problem-solving tasks and simulations give much more control to the learner. There is little doubt that the types of communicative tasks which have been developed for second and foreign language learning are intended to change the balance of power in the learner's direction. (Whether, in fact, these intentions are realised is another matter.)

Authority, power and control have become major issues with the rise of communicative language teaching. When we ask learners to communicate in a language over which they have only partial control, we are asking them to take risks which many of them may feel unhappy about. For many older learners, particularly those who have learned other second languages in classrooms where traditional approaches prevailed, the fact that they are asked to extemporise in a language over which they have only rudimentary control is extremely threatening.

4.4 Roles in the communicative classroom

The development of communicative language teaching has had a dramatic effect on the roles that learners are required to adopt. This is particularly true of oral interaction tasks. In the small-group interaction tasks which we have looked at in previous chapters, learners are required to put language to a range of uses, to use language which has been imperfectly mastered, to negotiate meaning, in short, to draw on their own resources rather than simply repeating and absorbing language. This can sometimes cause problems if you are teaching learners who have rather set ideas about language and learning, particularly if these differ greatly from your own. In such cases, you have a number of options. In the first instance you can insist that, as teacher, you know best and the learners must resign themselves to doing as you say. Alternatively, you can give in to the learners and structure activities around their preferences (assuming all learners think alike!). A more positive option would be to discuss the issue with the learners, explain why you want them to engage in communicative tasks, and attempt to come to a compromise.

While the practice of explaining and rationalising this to learners may seem a rather weak solution to the problem, it has proved useful in a number of contexts. For example, 'Sally', a teacher who was worried about her students' reluctance to engage in pair work, decided to try negotiating with her students to avoid a revolt over the use of role play and reported that:

> At first [the students] were a bit stunned and amused at the teacher wanting them to give their opinions on content and methodology. . . . As a result of the consultation process, all learners were quite prepared to continue with the pair work. Clarifying the rationale also made 'an incredible difference' to how they went about their pair work.
>
> (Nunan 1987: 70–1)

The roles of teachers and learners are, in many ways, complementary. Giving the learners a different role (such as greater initiative in the classroom) requires the teacher to adopt a different role. According to Breen and Candlin (1980), the teacher has three main roles in the communicative classroom. The first is to act as facilitator of the communicative process, the second is to act as a participant, and the third is to act as an observer and learner (Breen and Candlin 1980).

> Do you agree with this assertion? If not, which roles do you think the teacher can/should adopt?

Classroom interactions

The two extracts which follow are taken from lessons in which the focus is on oral interaction. However the roles which the learners play are quite different. What differences can you discern in the roles of teachers and learners in these two extracts?

LESSON I

Teacher: Stephen's Place, OK. So Myer's is on the corner. Here's the corner, OK. One corner is here, and one corner is here. Two corners, OK. Can you all see the corners? Understand the corner? Can you all see the corners? This is a corner, and this is a corner here, OK? One, two. And here is the corner of the table.

Student: And here?
Teacher: Corner, yes.
Student: Corner, yeah?
Teacher: OK Maria, where is the corner of your desk?
Student: Desk?
Teacher: Your desk.
Student: This one, this one.
Teacher: Corner? Your desk, yes, one corner.
Student: Here.
Teacher: Four corners.
Student: Oh, four.
Teacher: Yeah, four corners. Right, one . . .
Student: One, two, (two) three (three) four.
Teacher: Four, four corners, yeah, on the desk. Good. OK, And where's one corner of the room? Point to one corner. Yeah, that's one corner. Yes. Another one – two, yeah. Hung, three? Francey, four. Down on the ground. Yeah, four corners.

LESSON 2

Student: China, my mother is a teacher and my father is a teacher. Oh, she go finish, by bicycle, er, go to . . .
Student: House?
Student: No house, go to . . .
Student: School?
Student: My mother . . .
Teacher: Mmm
Student: . . . go to her mother.
Teacher: Oh, your grandmother.
Students: Grandmother.
Student: My grandmother. Oh, yes, by bicycle, by bicycle, oh, is, em, accident (gestures).
Teacher: In water?
Student: In water, yeah.
Teacher: In a river!
Student: River, yeah, river. Oh, yes, um, dead.
Students: Dead! Dead! Oh!

In Extract 1, the teacher plays the part of ringmaster. He asks the questions (most of which are 'display' questions which require the learners to provide answers which the teacher already knows). The only student-initiated interaction is on a point of vocabulary.

In the second extract, the learners have a much more active role. They communicate directly with each other, rather than exclusively with the teacher as is the case in Extract 1, and one student is allowed to take on the role of provider of content. During the interaction it is the learner who is the 'expert' and the teacher who is the 'learner' or follower.

From time to time, it is a good idea to record and analyse interactions in your own classroom. These interactions can either be between you and your students, or between students as they interact in small-group work. If you do, you may be surprised at the disparity between what you thought at the time was happening, and what actually took place as recorded on the tape. You should not be disconcerted if you do find such a disparity. In my experience, virtually all teachers, even the most experienced, discover dimensions to the lesson which they were unaware of at the time the lesson took place. (These will not all be negative, of course.)

The raw data of interaction, as above, are often illuminating. The following reactions were provided by a group of language teachers at an inservice workshop. The teachers had recorded, transcribed and analysed a lesson which they had recently given and were asked (among other things) to report back on what they had discovered about their own teaching, and about the insights they had gained into aspects of class-room management and interaction. Most of the comments referred, either explicitly or implicitly, to teacher/learner roles:

'As teachers we share an anxiety about "dominating" and so a common assumption that we are too intrusive, directive etc.'
'I need to develop skills for responding to the unexpected and exploit this to realise the full potential of the lesson.'
'There are umpteen aspects which need improving. There is also the effort of trying to respond to contradictory notions about teaching (e.g. intervention versus non-intervention).'
'I had been making a conscious effort to be non-directive, but was far more directive than I had thought.'
'Using small groups and changing groups can be perplexing and counter-productive, or helpful and stimulating. There is a need to plan carefully to make sure such changes are positive.'
'I have come to a better realisation of how much listening the teacher needs to do.'
'The teacher's role in facilitating interaction is extremely important for all types of classes. How do you teach teachers this?'
'I need to be more aware of the assumptions underlying my practice.'
'I discovered that I was over-directive and dominant.'
'Not to worry about periods of silence in the classroom.'
'I have a dreadful tendency to overload.'
'I praise students, but it is rather automatic. There is also a lot of teacher talk in my lessons.'
'I give too many instructions.'

'I discovered that, while my own style is valuable, it leads me to view issues in a "blinkered" way. I need to analyse my own and others' styles and ask why do I do it that way?'

In what ways are some of the issues dealt with earlier in the chapter reflected in these comments?

4.5 Roles and teaching materials

An examination of published materials can reveal just how rich and diverse teacher/learner roles can be. The following extracts have been taken from the introductions to a number of published coursebooks.

You might like to consider what learner/teacher roles are implied in the extracts, and also what similarities and differences there are between the extracts. Which coursebooks do you think have been specifically written from a communicative perspective?

1. Under guidance of the kind provided here, the student can proceed at his or her own speed, benefiting from the chance to work privately – and writing is a private art – as well as, one hopes, the opportunity to consult a tutor regularly. Additionally, the format of the units, with their detailed answer sections, enables a tutor to look after anything from one to thirty students simultaneously, without getting flooded out with material to correct. Traditional writing courses can be very hard on the tutor. This one is not.

   Not everything in the exercises has been explained in the instructions, partly because such a procedure would have made the course too bulky, and partly because it is natural and desirable that students should induce as much as possible by themselves. Since creative expression is very much a personal thing, however, it has been assumed that teachers can encourage the free development of writing skills, and also that a professional person can divert what he or she has learnt into the channels of special interest without further help from us.

   (McArthur 1984: 10–11)

2. We believe that students learn a lot by working together in groups to solve a problem or make a decision. We feel that learners should share their knowledge, compare their opinions,

and discuss their ideas in small groups before going on to classwork or individual work. The instructions for each exercise include suggestions about ways of working with the material. However, these are only suggestions, and different teachers and classes will adjust them to their own ideas and circumstances.

(Coe, Rycroft, and Ernest 1983: 4)

3. The student must be trained adequately in all four basic language skills: understanding, speaking, reading and writing. In many classroom courses the emphasis is wholly on the written language. The student is trained to use his eyes instead of his ears and his inability to achieve anything like correct pronunciation, stress and intonation must be attributed largely to the tyranny of the printed word. If the teacher is to train his students in all four skills, he must make efficient use of the time at his disposal. Efficiency presupposes the adoption of classroom procedures which will yield the best results in the quickest possible time.

(Alexander 1967: viii)

4. *Images* is ideally suited for use by beginning students in a multi-level classroom, or for independent practice and study in the language lab or home. The method is simple and easily grasped by a non-English speaking student. Lesson 1 assumes no previous knowledge of English. The visual format makes the mode of progression through the book self-explanatory, and a minimal amount of demonstration will get a student started in the program.

   Each lesson opens with a photo presentation introducing the new functions, vocabulary and structures. The student begins by reading the photo presentation and listening to the conversation or narration on the tape cassette. He or she repeats the dialogue lines after the actors, practicing pronunciation and inflection.

(Zuern 1985: Introduction)

4.6 Settings

'Settings' refers to the classroom arrangements specified or implied in the task, and it also requires consideration of whether the task is to be carried out wholly or partly outside the classroom. While some might prefer that roles and settings be dealt with separately, I have decided to deal with them together, as the social setting (whether, for example, an activity involves the whole class, small groups or individuals) will be an important factor influencing roles and relationships.

The following diagram from Wright (1987) illustrates the different ways in which learners might be grouped physically or arranged within the classroom.

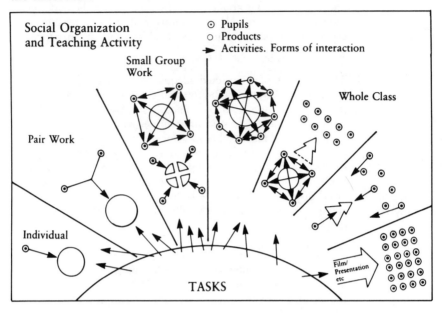

Wright: Roles of Teachers and Learners, p. 58

In their discussion of listening tasks, Anderson and Lynch (1988) suggest that:

> One aspect of the classroom listening context that is independent of the language input is the decision whether to adopt a format of group or individual work. The same message can be played either to individual listeners or to groups for discussion. The latter method is attractive for a number of reasons. . . . We might wish to use group-based work for general pedagogic reasons, such as a belief in the importance of increasing the cooperation and cohesiveness among students. Then there are more specifically language oriented arguments: classroom researchers such as Pica and Doughty (1985) have offered evidence for the positive role of group work in promoting a linguistic environment likely to assist L2 learning.

(Anderson and Lynch 1988: 59)

Nunan (1985), distinguishes between two different aspects of the learning situation. He refers to these as 'mode' and 'environment'. Learning mode refers to whether the learner is operating on an individual or group basis. If operating on an individual basis, is the learner self-paced but teacher directed, or self-directed? If the learner is operating as part of a group, is the task for mostly whole class, small group or pair work? Each of these configurations has implications for task design.

Environment, which is closely connected with mode, refers to where the learning actually takes place. It might be a conventional classroom in a language centre, a community class, an industrial or occupational setting, a self-access learning centre and so on. Until comparatively recently, it was assumed that learning would take place inside a conventional classroom. However, in many educational institutions, particularly those catering for adult learners, more flexible arrangements and options are being experimented with.

One particularly interesting experiment has been the direct use of the wider community as a resource for learning. Here, learners spend as much time out of the classroom as they do in it, collecting information and language data relating to particular themes or issues and interacting with native speakers as they do so. Strevens (1987: 171) suggests that tasks which use the community as a resource have three particular benefits:

1. they provide learners with opportunities for genuine interactions which have a real-life point to them;
2. learners can adopt communicative roles which bypass the teacher as intermediary;
3. they can change the in-class role relationships between teacher and pupils.

Montgomery and Eisenstein (1982) gave a strong real-world focus to their classroom by organising instruction around a series of weekly excursions. Venues were selected on the basis of learner interest and need. Montgomery and Eisenstein found that the community-based learning experiences were highly successful, not only in terms of student interest but also in terms of language gain.

> Consider your own approach to classroom tasks. Which student configurations do you favour? You might like to think about why you favour some ways of organising learners rather than others. What opportunities are there, if any, for using the wider community as a resource for learning?
> You might like to think about why you favour some patterns over others.

4.7 Conclusion

In Chapter 4, we have looked at the roles for teachers and learners which are implicit in various tasks. We have seen that roles can vary quite markedly, and that the roles which are established can have a marked bearing on the language which learners produce. We have also seen that an investigation of roles need not be confined to aural/oral tasks, but can be extended to reading and writing tasks as well. In all macroskills, changing roles reflect the theoretical and methodological shifts which have been taking place within the profession.

Of course, much more can be said about learner and teacher roles. A large body of literature exists on the application of principles of humanistic education to language teaching and learning, and this literature is largely concerned with redefining learner and teacher roles.

One particular aspect of humanistic education which has attracted a good deal of interest in recent years has been the incorporation of learner-centred principles into the language classroom. In a learner-centred curriculum, information by and about learners is built into every stage of the curriculum process. This involvement of the learner in curriculum, planning, implementation and evaluation requires the adoption of new roles by all those involved in curriculum processes, but particularly on the part of teacher and learners. Teachers have to accept that learners have a right to have their views incorporated into the selection of content and learning experiences, and need to provide learners with the appropriate opportunities for them to make choices. Learners, for their part, need to develop a range of skills related not only to language, but also to learning and learning-how-to-learn. (For a detailed exploration of learner-centred principles in language teaching see Nunan 1988.)

In the next chapter, we turn from a focus on the components of a task to the important issue of grading tasks.

References and further reading

Alexander, L. 1967. *Practice and Progress Part 2*. London: Longman.

Anderson, A., and T. Lynch. 1988. *Listening*. Oxford: Oxford University Press.

Bell, J., and B. Burnaby. 1984. *A Handbook for ESL Literacy*. Toronto: OISE.

Breen, M., and C. Candlin. 1980. The essentials of a communicative curriculum in language teaching. *Applied Linguistics*, 1 (2), 89–112.

Candlin, C., and D. Nunan. 1987. *Revised Syllabus Specifications for the Omani School English Language Curriculum*. Muscat: Ministry of Education and Youth.

Carnicelli, T. 1980. The writing conference: a one-to-one conversation. In

T. Donovan and B. McClelland (Eds.). *Eight Approaches to Teaching Conversation*. Urbana Ill.: National Council of Teachers of English.

Clarke, M., and S. Silberstein. 1977. Toward a realization of psycholinguistic principles in the ESL reading class. *Language Learning*, 27 (1), 48–65.

Coe, N., R. Rycroft, and P. Ernest. 1983. *Writing Skills: A Problem-Solving Approach*. Cambridge: Cambridge University Press.

Comeau, R. 1987. Interactive oral grammar exercises. In Rivers.

Dickinson, L. 1987. *Self-instruction in Language Learning*. Cambridge: Cambridge University Press.

Dubin, F., and E. Olshtain. 1986. *Course Design: Developing Programs and Materials for Language Learning*. Cambridge: Cambridge University Press.

McArthur, T. 1984. *The Written Word: A Course in Controlled Composition*. Oxford: Oxford University Press.

Montgomery, C., and M. Eisenstein. 1982. Real reality revisited: An experimental communicative course in ESL. *TESOL Quarterly*, 19, 2.

Nunan, D. 1985. *Language Teaching Course Design: Trends and Issues*. Adelaide: National Curriculum Resource Centre.

Nunan, D. 1987. *The Teacher as Curriculum Developer*. Adelaide: National Curriculum Resource Centre.

Nunan, D. 1988. *The Learner-Centred Curriculum*. Cambridge: Cambridge University Press.

Pica, T., and C. Doughty. 1985. The role of groupwork in classroom second language acquisition. *Studies in Second Language Acquisition*, 7, 233–48.

Richards, J., and T. Rodgers. 1986. *Approaches and Methods in Language Teaching*. Cambridge: Cambridge University Press.

Rivers, W. (Ed.) 1987. *Interactive Language Teaching*. Cambridge: Cambridge University Press.

Rubin, J., and I. Thompson. 1982. *The Good Language Learner*. Boston Mass.: Heinle and Heinle.

Rutherford, W. 1987. *Second Language Grammar: Learning and Teaching*. London: Longman.

Strevens, P. 1987. Interaction outside the classroom: using the community. In Rivers.

Willing, K. 1988. *Learning Styles in Adult Migrant Education*. Adelaide: National Curriculum Resource Centre.

Wright, T. 1987. *Roles of Teachers and Learners*. Oxford: Oxford University Press.

Zamel, V. 1982. Writing: the process of discovering meaning. *TESOL Quarterly*, 16 (2) 495–9.

Zuern, G. 1985. *Images 1*. Reading Ma.: Addison-Wesley.

5 Grading tasks

5.1 Introduction

We have now looked at what a language task is, what its distinctive components are, and what roles a task might imply for teacher and learner. We have looked at a number of task types in relation to both separate and integrated language skills. In so far as the methodology/ syllabus design distinction is useful, our emphasis has so far been on the former.

However, in Chapter 1 I made the claim that the task has an important part to play in curriculum planning that embraced both the how and the what of a language learning programme. If the notion of task is to have value in compiling a learning programme – and I have indicated that from the viewpoint of both teacher and learner it would seem to hold this promise – then we have to cater for three key concepts in syllabus design: grading, sequencing and integrating. This chapter and the next address these questions.

If you examine a selection of coursebooks, you will find that the content has been graded in different ways. The grammatical list in *Checkpoint English* for example, introduces 'subject pronouns' and 'the verb "be"' in Unit 1 while 'regular past simple' and 'possessive pronouns' and 'adjectives' are postponed until Unit 9. In *Exchanges* 'opinions' and 'arguments' are introduced in Unit 3 while 'explanations' and 'instructions' are not introduced until Unit 8. Decisions on what to teach first, what second, and what last in a coursebook or programme will reflect the beliefs of the coursebook writer or syllabus designer about grading.

Grading has been described in the following way:

> the arrangement of the content of a language course or a textbook so that it is presented in a helpful way. Gradation would affect the order in which words, word meanings, tenses, structures, topics, functions, skills, etc. are presented. Gradation may be based on the complexity of an item, its frequency in written or spoken English, or its importance for the learner.
>
> (Richards, Platt, and Weber 1986: 125)

In other words, the content in Week 1 of a language course is selected either because it is easy, or because it occurs frequently, or because the learner needs it rather urgently for real-world communication. (See also Wilkins 1976 for a detailed treatment of grading.)

The grading of content for a language programme is an extremely complicated and difficult business, even for syllabus designers who have had a great deal of experience. In this chapter we shall only be able to deal with some of the more important factors involved.

It is sometimes suggested that grading content was a relatively straight-forward business in the days when that content was largely restricted to grammar. In fact, determining what is grammatically easy or difficult is not quite as straightforward as it might seem. This is partly due to the fact that measurement of grammatical ease and difficulty will vary according to which grammatical system you happen to be following. It is further complicated by the fact that what is easy from the perspective of grammatical analysis is not necessarily that which will be easy to learn, a fact which has been demonstrated by second language acquisition research. For example, Pienemann and Johnston (1987) have been able to demonstrate that while the rule for using the third person singular 's' is fairly simple in terms of grammatical analysis, in terms of speech processing (i.e. the load it places on the learner's short-term memory) it is quite difficult.

If deciding which grammatical items are easy or difficult presents problems, things become much more complicated once we look at the grading of tasks. This is because there are so many different factors to be taken into consideration.

Here, I shall consider factors in relation to the various components in our model of task. I shall be particularly concerned with factors relating to input, activities and the learner. While goal factors are important, I shall not give them separate consideration here as they relate closely to the factors implicated in the difficulty of activities and are, in any case, difficult to describe without a detailed description of the programme from which they are derived.

In the next three sections, we shall look in some detail at the factors involved in determining difficulty from the perspective of inputs, learners and activities.

5.2 Input factors

In this section, we shall look at those factors in listening or reading task inputs which are likely to cause difficulty.

The first thing to consider is the complexity of the text. This will be affected by grammatical factors. A text consisting of simple sentences will generally be considered easier than one which contains non-finite verb phrases and subordination. For example, Sentence A will be immediately recognised as less complex than Sentence B.

> You might like to list those factors which make Sentence B more complex than Sentence A.

Sentence A:
The boy went home.

Sentence B:
Having insufficient money, the boy, who wanted to go to the cinema, went home instead.

Actually, we need to be careful here. It has been found that rewriting texts so that they are simpler grammatically can actually make them more difficult to comprehend. Consider, for example, the following passages:

Passage A:
The pupils fooled around because the teacher left the room.

Passage B:
The teacher left the room. The pupils fooled around.

Question:
Why did the pupils fool around?

Learners reading the more grammatically complex passage (Passage A) will, all other things being equal, actually find the comprehension question easier to answer than those reading Passage B. This is because the cause/effect relationship in Passage A is explicitly marked by the conjunction 'because' whereas readers of Passage B will have to infer the relationship.

In addition to grammatical complexity, difficulty will be affected by the length of the text, the propositional density (how much information it contains and the extent to which this information is recycled), the amount of low frequency vocabulary, the speed of spoken texts and the number of speakers involved, the explicitness of the information, the discourse structure and the clarity with which this is signalled (for example paragraphs in which the main point is buried away will probably be more difficult to process than those in which the main idea is clearly presented in the opening sentence). In addition, it has been found that a passage in which the information is presented in the same chronological order as it occurred in real life is easier to process than one in which the information is presented out of sequence (Brown and Yule 1983).

The amount of support provided to the listener or reader will also have a bearing on textual difficulty. A passage with headings and sub-headings which is supported with photographs, drawings, tables, graphs and so on should be easier to process than one in which there is no contextual support. (I have used 'should' advisedly. The extent to which all these factors do promote comprehension needs to be determined empirically.)

There are, in fact, many studies into the comprehensibility of modified and unmodified versions of aural and written texts. One such study, by Parker and Chaudron (1987), compared the comprehensibility of an elaborated written text with a non-elaborated version. They found that the elaborated text did not lead to lower comprehensibility as measured by a cloze test. However, they also point out that more research is needed into the effect of interaction, elaboration and simplification on the comprehensibility of aural and written texts.

The importance of having a framework to assist in comprehension can be illustrated with the following story.

> You might like to try reading the story then closing the book and recalling as much of the information in the passage as you can.

> If the balloons popped, the sound wouldn't be able to carry since everything would be too far away from the correct floor. A closed window would prevent the sound from carrying, since most buildings tend to be well insulated. Since the whole operation depends on a steady flow of electricity, a break in the middle of the wire would also cause problems. Of course, the fellow could shout, but the human voice is not loud enough to carry that far. An additional problem is that a wire could break on the instrument. Then there could be no accompaniment to the message. It is clear that the best situation would involve less distance. Then there would be fewer potential problems. With face-to-face contact, the least number of things could go wrong.
>
> (Bransford and Johnson 1972: 717)

Most people find they have a great deal of difficulty remembering much of the story at all.

The story was used in a well-known experiment by Bransford and Johnson (1972) who found that subjects who heard the story as it appears above understood very little. However, subjects who were given an accompanying picture to provide a context recalled most of the story. This picture showed a man serenading his girlfriend on an electric guitar. The girl was in a high-rise apartment, and the man got his message to her by suspending a loud-speaker from a bunch of balloons.

> Try the story again now that you have the clues.

Finally, the type or 'genre' of text will have an effect on its difficulty. Brown and Yule (1983) suggest that descriptions will be simpler than instructions which, in turn, will be easier than stories. Abstract discussions, or those involving the expression of opinions and attitudes, will be more difficult still.

Compare the following passages and rank them according to their likely difficulty for intermediate level ESL readers. Can you identify which features or characteristics (i.e. vocabulary, grammar, genre etc.) are responsible for text difficulty, or do these various features interact to cause difficulty?

PASSAGE A:

The boy felt his way up the creaking stairs through thick darkness, his eyes raised to the faint moonlight that shone along the landing. He stopped as the great clock below whirred for a few seconds and gave out a single, solemn stroke. He hesitated as the sound died down and then crept on, thinking that if they could sleep through that, they would sleep through any noise he could make. All he had to do was get past that central door on the landing; he was just telling himself he was safe when the door was flung open and the gaunt old man grabbed him by the shoulder.

(Robinson 1977: 80)

PASSAGE B:

Sound travels at 760 miles per hour, and in the early years of aviation it must have seemed to many that aircraft would always be confined to subsonic speeds by the inexorable laws of nature. However, aircraft speed was increased by constant improvements, until, shortly after the Second World War, the first aircraft were built which were capable of speeds faster than that of sound.

High speeds presented designers with problems of three kinds, which had to be solved before regular supersonic flights could be considered feasible.

(Robinson 1977: 118)

PASSAGE C:

Redundancy is a matter of increasing concern to managers and to professional people who work for companies. The complexity of modern industry means that 'executives' now constitute a larger proportion of a firm's population than before, so that reorganisations of management structure make their jobs more precarious than they were in the past. Financial compensation for redundancy is provided under the law, but money does not compensate for the satisfaction that many such people get from their work and of which redundancy deprives them, so that they have considerable problems to face. There are of course wide differences among redundant managers in personality, age, social and family background and reemployment prospects, so that individuals react in varying ways, but few go through the experience with equanimity and for most it is an ordeal.

(Robinson 1977: 129)

PASSAGE D:

'The Game is Forever', by Jonathan Frost, at the Minuscule Theatre. Last night's first night of Mr Frost's play at the Minuscule was a memorable event in my career as a critic, setting new records in the stimulation of foot-shuffling and eye-rolling, in the production of groans, both suppressed and uttered, and in the intensity of the desire it engendered to quit the scene of torture. But I must be calm; it's all over now, the threat implied in the title was mercifully not fulfilled and it is my duty to tell you what happened. A great deal, indeed far too much, was said and done on the stage last night, but nothing can be said to have happened.

(Robinson 1977: 121)

The four passages have all been taken from the same book. However, they are not all of the same order of difficulty. Not only do they vary in terms of linguistic complexity (for example in terms of grammar and vocabulary), but they also vary in terms of text type (for example narrative versus satirical review) and topic.

In considering topic, it is generally assumed that abstract topics, such as 'redundancy' will pose greater problems for the reader than concrete topics, such as 'speed'. However, the extent of such problems will depend on the extent of the learner's background knowledge of the topic in question. It may well be that an unfamiliar concrete topic will pose greater problems than a familiar abstract topic.

The role of the learner in relation to task difficulty is an important one and it is to the learner that we now turn.

5.3 Learner factors

In their book on reading comprehension, Pearson and Johnson (1972) distinguish between what they call 'inside the head' factors and 'outside the head' factors. 'Outside the head' factors include those things we have already discussed in 5.2. In 5.4 we shall look at more of these.

'Inside the head' factors include all of those things which the learner brings to the task of understanding and using language. Pearson and

Johnson suggest that comprehension is a process of building bridges between the known and the unknown. In other words, we start with a knowledge framework and attempt to fit new information into it. In those cases where the new information will not fit into our pre-existing framework, we may have to modify the framework itself.

We can illustrate this as follows. When reading or listening to a story set in a restaurant, we call up our mental restaurant 'map' to help us understand the story. This map is a composite made from all our previous restaurant experiences. If these experiences have been restricted to four star restaurants, and the story we are reading/listening to is set in a Macdonald's Hamburger Bar, we may have difficulty comprehending some of the things that are going on. (For example, we may have difficulty working out why the customers go first to a counter rather than having their order taken by a waiter/waitress.) As a result of reading/ listening to the story, we may have to change our restaurant 'map' to accommodate several new pieces of information.

Brindley suggests that, in addition to background knowledge, learner factors will include confidence, motivation, learning pace, observed ability in language skills, cultural knowledge/awareness and linguistic knowledge. He proposes a list of questions which need to be considered in relation to each of these factors. These are as follows:

Confidence:
— How confident does the learner have to be to carry out the task?
— Does the learner have the necessary level of confidence?
Motivation:
— How motivating is the task?
Prior learning experience:
— Does the task assume familiarity with certain learning skills?
— Does the learner's prior learning experience provide the necessary learning skills/strategies to carry out the task?
Learning pace:
— How much learning material has the learner shown s/he is capable of handling?
— Is the task broken down into manageable parts?
Observed ability in language skills:
— What is the learner's assessed ability in the skills concerned?
— Does this assessment conform to his/her observed behaviour in class?
— In the light of the teacher's assessment, what overall level of performance can reasonably be expected?
Cultural knowledge/awareness:
— Does the task assume cultural knowledge?

— If so, can the learner be expected to have it?
— Does the task assume knowledge of a particular subject?
Linguistic knowledge:
— How much linguistic knowledge does the learner have?
— What linguistic knowledge is assumed by the task?

Which of these factors do you think are most likely to be of relevance when considering task difficulty in relation to your own students?

As we have already noted, input and learner factors are not always independent. There will be an interaction between the grammatical complexity of the input, and the learner's level of linguistic knowledge. The problem for the teacher or materials developer is in judging just how much linguistic and background knowledge the learner is likely to have. Pearson and Johnson have described this problem as follows:

> [there is an interdependence] between inside the head and outside the head factors. Text readability really boils down to linguistic factors like word difficulty (how familiar are the words?) and sentence complexity (how difficult is it to wade through coordinated and subordinated text segments?). Hence, one cannot know how difficult a text will be until and unless one knows something about the linguistic and conceptual sophistication of the reader: one person's *Scientific American* is another person's daily newspaper. In short, all of these factors interact with one another.
>
> (Pearson and Johnson 1972: 10)

The assumptions made by a speaker or writer about the cultural knowledge possessed by the listener or reader can have an important effect on the ability of the second language learner to comprehend a text. A number of studies have shown that the ability of learners to comprehend texts can be adversely affected by the cultural assumptions they make. For example, Nunan (1985) found that the lack of appropriate background knowledge was a more significant factor in the ability of second language learners to comprehend school texts than linguistic complexity as measured by various readability formulae.

There is a problem for the teacher or materials writer wanting to accommodate the learner's cultural knowledge or lack of knowledge.

How would you determine what background knowledge learners might or might not have?

5.4 Activity factors

The final set of factors I wish to consider are those associated with the activities themselves.

In recent years, with the increasing use of authentic texts, there has been a tendency to control difficulty not by simplifying the input to which learners are exposed, but by varying the difficulty of the activities which learners are expected to carry out.

This principle of holding the input constant and varying the activities can be illustrated with the following example from Jones and Moar (1985) which is based on an extract from an authentic radio broadcast.

UNIT 9 — WHAT'S ON?

Now what's happening this weekend?

Well first of all I have to apologize because last weekend everything I said was on wasn't because of the rain.

Ah, the Model Toy Exhibition at Paradise Gardens last Sunday was rescheduled for this coming Sunday.

The Gala Fete at the Spastic Centre is now going to be held later in June.

But this weekend you can see an Orchid Show at the Dee Why R.S.L. and a Gem Show at the Lindfield Masonic Hall.

You can go to the Ski Show at the overseas shipping terminal and something called Craft Expo at the Hyatt Kingsgate Hotel. All of those events are undercover so they will take place whatever happens to the rain. Mike Bailey tells us there is an excellent chance of fine weather on Sunday and I hope he's right because on Sunday you can walk for the Spastic Centre or you can run for the Multiple Sclerosis Society of N.S.W. and if you're very fast you can do both.

A 10km walk starts at 9.30 at the amphitheatre in Martin Place. The Fun Run begins at Pier I at noon. And finally I just want to tell you there's a new play in town. It's at the New Theatre in Newtown (there's a lot of News there). I haven't yet seen it but it sounds so fascinating that I'm going to try and get along there tonight.

It's about a day in the life of a major suburban newspaper when the owner comes to visit and it's called "Waiting for Rupert Murdoch".

It's at the New Theatre at Newtown. And that's my lot for today.

Jones and Moar: Listen to Australia, p. 126

WHAT'S ON?

*ACTIVITY 1

Listen to the tape.

What does the announcer say about the weather? Tick ☑ the right answers.

WHAT'S ON?

**ACTIVITY 1
Listen to the tape.
What does the announcer say you can do this weekend? Tick ☑ the ones you hear.

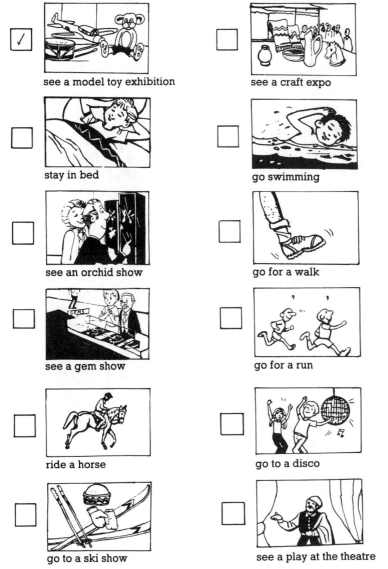

✓ see a model toy exhibition	☐ see a craft expo
☐ stay in bed	☐ go swimming
☐ see an orchid show	☐ go for a walk
☐ see a gem show	☐ go for a run
☐ ride a horse	☐ go to a disco
☐ go to a ski show	☐ see a play at the theatre

WHAT'S ON?

***ACTIVITY 1

(a)   Write the names of these weekend activities under the pictures.

- go to a play
- a walkathon
- an orchid show
- a model toy exhibition

- a ski show
- a gem show
- a craft expo
- a fun run

_____

_____

_____

_____

_____

_____

_____

_____

(b)   Listen to the tape.

Using the boxes, number 1 — 8 the activities as you hear them.

ibid, p. 101

> Do you agree with the authors on the relative difficulty
> of these activities? What are the factors determining ease
> and difficulty (i.e. why is activity 2 more difficult than
> activity 1, and activity 3 more difficult than activities 1
> and 2?)

Brindley (1987) suggests that the following factors will determine the
complexity of what the learner has to do:

Relevance:
– Is the task meaningful and relevant to the learner?
Complexity:
– How many steps are involved in the task?
– How complex are the instructions?
– What cognitive demands does the task make on the learner?
– How much information is the learner expected to process in
  performing the task?
Amount of context provided prior to task:
– How much prior knowledge of the world, the situation or the
  cultural context is assumed in the way the task is framed?
– How much preliminary activity is allowed for to introduce the task
  and set the context?
Processability of language of the task:
– Is the language that learners are expected to produce in line with
  their processing capacity?
Amount of help available to the learner:
– How much assistance can the learner get from the teacher, other
  learners, books or other learning aids?
– In the case of interactive tasks, is the interlocutor sympathetic, does
  he/she provide help?
– What is his/her tolerance level to non-standard language?
Degree of grammatical accuracy/contextual appropriacy:
– How 'standard' does the task require learners to be?
– What is the desired effect on the interlocutor?
– Does he/she expect or demand accuracy?
Time available to the learner:
– How long does the learner have to carry out the task?

> Do you agree that all these factors mentioned by
> Brindley relate to the activity (or, as he calls it, 'task'), or
> should some more properly belong to the input or
> learner categories?

Candlin and Nunan (1987) have also suggested that activities can be
graded according to the general cognitive demands they make. Their
scheme, which has been adapted from Bruner, has four levels as follows:

1. *Attending and recognising*
   Here we mean the learner's ability to notice what kind of
   input/experience he or she is being confronted with. The ability
   to recognise that it is an example of language.

2. *Making sense*
   Here we mean the learner's ability to make sense of the input as
   a particular example of language, determining, for example,
   what particular language it is, what features it has, how it is
   organised and structured, how it is classified and patterned.

3. *Going beyond the information given*
   Here we mean the learner's ability to go beyond the immediate
   surface information of the text, hypothesising, inferring and
   making judgements, for example, about the underlying
   meanings of the text, its purposes and its author and audience.

4. *Transferring and generalising*
   Here we mean the learner's ability to extrapolate from any
   particular texts of the same type, genre and purpose, or
   transferring the information gained from and about a particular
   text to other texts that may be of other quite different structure,
   channel and purpose. Here also we emphasise the ability to
   collate and recode information, and seek corroboration through
   feedback.

(Candlin and Nunan 1987)

In this list, complexity is a function of the cognitive operations the learner
has to perform. In the list which follows, cognitive operations are only
one of the factors involved.

> Study the following list from Candlin (1987) and note
> which factors relate to input, which to the learner and
> which to the activity.

Cognitive load:
It will be difficult easily to distinguish what is cognitively difficult for learners to accomplish from what is communicatively difficult. Nonetheless, we may be able to design tasks in which there is a gradual increase in cognitive complexity without dramatically raising the communicative load. For example, tasks which require learners to follow a clear chronological sequence, referring to individual actions of individual characters, will clearly be cognitively less demanding than a task in which there is no such clear development and where the picture is complicated by multiple actions and multiple actors.

Communicative stress:
Brown and Yule (1983) offer a description of the most complex situation that a non-native speaker of a language might be expected to face: where he or she has to converse on a topic known more to his/her interlocutor than him/herself, where there is more than one such interlocutor, where the interlocutors are more communicatively competent, where the interlocutors know more about the subject-matter, where the communicative task does not follow a clear structured organisation but focuses on reasons for actions rather than actions themselves.

Particularity and generalisability:
Tasks which follow some generalised pattern, say of assembling components, are easier to manage than those where the order of assembly or the norms of interpretation are unclear or to be negotiated. For example, asking someone original questions about hypothesised future events is likely to pose a more difficult task than the recounting of familiar experience.

Code complexity and interpretive density:
We might want to play off linguistic complexity against task difficulty; e.g. we might want, with linguistically elaborate texts, to ask more straightforward questions, while with simple texts asking questions which required interpretive and explanatory analysis on the part of the learner.

Process continuity:
Learners should be encouraged to create their own continuity and sequencing by examining what needs to be known and experienced before a more complex task can be achieved.

(Adapted from Candlin 1987: 19–20)

The last point raised by Candlin, on the desirability of sequencing tasks so that one logically follows another, raises the issue of task 'dependency', which we shall discuss in the next chapter.

Prabhu provides a slightly different perspective on task complexity. Experience on the Bangalore Project suggested that the following factors were the most significant ones in determining difficulty:

1. *Information provided*
   The amount and type of information handled will affect difficulty.
2. *Reasoning needed*
   The number of steps or cognitive operations (e.g. deduction, inference or calculation) will affect difficulty.
3. *Precision needed*
   Difficulty increases with the degree of precision called for.
4. *Familiarity with constraints*
   Learners' knowledge of the world and familiarity with purposes and constraints will affect difficulty.
5. *Degree of abstractness*
   Working with concepts is more difficult than working with the names of objects or actions.

(Prabhu 1987: 87–8)

How are these general approaches realised in practice? Here is an example of a distinction of learning levels adapted from a syllabus for children learning English as a foreign language. Study the lists. Do you agree that the activities become increasingly difficult? See whether you can determine which factors have been used by the syllabus designer in grading the activities.

GRADED ACTIVITY SPECIFICATIONS

Beginner

Social and interpersonal

- comprehend requests for personal information
- give personal details (name, age, address)
- write own name and names of class and family
- ask for personal information (name, age, address)
- take part in short, contextualised dialogues focusing on exchange of interpersonal information
- listen to short, interpersonal dialogue and identify number, age and gender of interlocutors
- sight read nametags for self and other class members
- inquire about and express capability and lack of capability

Informational

Instructive

- comprehend and carry out simple instructions relating to physical actions which can be carried out in the classroom e.g. point to, touch, stand up, sit down
- give simple instructions to other members of the class
- sight read contextualised public notices e.g. 'Stop!', 'Go!'

Descriptive

- listen to simple descriptions of common objects (i.e. those in the immediate environment) and people and identify these
- listen to short descriptive aural text and identify key words
- ask for the name of common objects inside and outside the classroom
- read 2–3 sentence descriptions of familiar objects and people
- give short aural description of familiar objects and people

Narrative

- listen to short narratives and identify key words
- comprehend gist of short narrative given appropriate contextual and non-verbal support

Affective

- recite songs and rhymes

Nunan: Syllabus Specifications

Pre-Intermediate

Social and interpersonal

- listen to a dialogue and identify discourse strategies
- comprehend and respond to requests for information about interests
- comprehend, respond to and make requests and offers

Informational

Instructive

- comprehend and carry out a linked sequence of instructions
- listen to a sequence of instructions and transform the information by completing a table, map, diagram etc.
- give a sequence of oral instructions to classmates

Descriptive

- identify core vocabulary items when encountered in aural and written descriptions
- listen to and read short descriptive texts and answer questions requiring the making of inferences
- read 2–3 paragraph descriptions and identify main idea
- write a short description of self and others
- give a short oral description of self and others
- identify antecedents to anaphoric reference items in written descriptions
- give a short oral or written description of a picture relating to topic areas

Narrative

- identify core vocabulary items when encountered in aural and written narratives
- listen to and read short descriptive texts and answer questions requiring the making of inferences
- grasp the gist of a short narrative, and demonstrate understanding by, e.g. numbering a set of pictures in appropriate sequence
- talk about future events
- describe a linked sequence of past events
- listen to or read a short narrative and predict what will happen next

Affective

- identify the emotional state of a speaker from tone and intonation.

Intermediate

Social and interpersonal

- use an appropriate conversational style
- use the following conversational strategies – seeking turns, holding the floor
- use appropriate non-verbal behaviour
- identify the relationship of participants in an aural interaction
- differentiate between fact and opinion in interpersonal interactions

Informational

Instructive

- follow an extended set of instructions
- give a set of aural and written instructions on how to make or assemble something

Descriptive

- grasp the gist of an extended aural description on a familiar topic
- initiate and respond to requests for facts, opinions and attitudes relating to aural and written descriptive texts
- read and integrate information presented textually and non-textually (i.e. as tables, graphs, charts etc.)
- comprehend marked logical relationships in aural and written texts

Narrative

- grasp the gist of an extended narrative
- comprehend the details of short narratives on unfamiliar topics
- extract specific information from aural and written narratives on familiar topics
- initiate and respond to requests for facts, opinions and attitudes relating to aural and written narrative texts
- retell narratives in own words (orally – in writing)

Affective

- listen to/read imaginative texts for pleasure
- write short imaginative text.

Grading tasks

A set of activities graded at seven levels of difficulty and sorted according to the four macroskills is included as Appendix C. This appendix has been included as a resource for you to draw on in developing your own activities. You might like to think about which factors have been taken into consideration in grading these.

5.5 Conclusion

In this chapter we have looked at some of the factors involved in grading language tasks. The issue of grading is an extremely complex one, and we have only scratched the surface. We have seen that there are many factors at work, all of which have a bearing on task complexity, but that most of these can be categorised according to whether they relate to inputs, learners or activities. Determining task complexity is made difficult, not only by the range of factors involved, but also by the interaction of these factors with each other. Thus the difficulty of a task based on a simple input text can be increased by setting activities which require different learner responses. The same learner response can be made more or less difficult by selection of input, or by making demands on learners' background knowledge.

In addition to the factors which we have looked at in this chapter, there are many others which will impinge on task difficulty. In particular, there are many learner factors, such as maturational level, which are difficult to discuss without reference to particular learner groups.

Despite the difficulties involved, as teachers we are constantly estimating the difficulty of the tasks which our learners undertake. In the final analysis, it might well be that it is the learners who impose their own automatic order of difficulty by doing and not doing what they can and cannot do.

References and further reading

Bransford, J., and M. Johnson. 1972. Contextual prerequisites for understanding: some investigations of comprehension and recall. *Journal of Verbal Learning and Verbal Recall*, 11, 717–26.

Brindley, G. 1987. Factors affecting task difficulty. In D. Nunan *Guidelines for the Development of Curriculum Resources*. Adelaide: National Curriculum Resource Centre.

Brown, G., and G. Yule. 1983. *Teaching the Spoken Language*. Cambridge: Cambridge University Press.

Candlin, C. 1987. Towards task-based language learning. In C. Candlin and D. Murphy (Eds.) *Language Learning Tasks*. Englewood Cliffs NJ: Prentice-Hall.

Candlin, C., and D. Nunan. 1987. *Revised Syllabus Specifications for the Omani School English Language Curriculum.* Muscat: Ministry of Education and Youth.

Jones, M., and R. Moar. 1985. *Listen to Australia.* Adelaide: National Curriculum Resource Centre.

Nunan, D. 1985. Content familiarity and the perception of textual relationships in second language reading. *RELC Journal,* 16 (1), 43–51.

Nunan, D. 1987. *Guidelines for the Development of Curriculum Resources.* Adelaide: National Curriculum Resource Centre.

Nunan, D. 1989. *Syllabus Specifications for the Omani School English Language Curriculum.* Sultanate of Oman: Ministry of Education and Youth.

Parker, K., and C. Chaudron. 1987. The effects of linguistic simplification and elaborative modifications on L2 comprehension. Manuscript.

Pearson, P. D., and D. D. Johnson. 1972. *Teaching Reading Comprehension.* New York: Holt, Rinehart and Winston.

Pienemann, M., and M. Johnston. 1987. Factors influencing the development of language proficiency. In D. Nunan (Ed.) *Applying Second Language Acquisition Research.* Adelaide: National Curriculum Resource Centre.

Prabhu, N. 1987. *Second Language Pedagogy: A Perspective.* Oxford: Oxford University Press.

Prowse, P., J. Garton-Sprenger, and T. C. Jupp. 1981. *Exchanges: Students' Book.* London: Heinemann.

Richards, J., J. Platt, and H. Weber. 1986. *Longman Dictionary of Applied Linguistics.* London: Longman.

Robinson, C. 1977. *Advanced Use of English: A Coursebook.* London: Hamish Hamilton.

Whitney, N. 1983. *Checkpoint English 1.* Oxford: Oxford University Press.

Wilkins, D. 1976. *Notional Syllabuses.* Oxford: Oxford University Press.

6 Sequencing and integrating tasks

6.1 Introduction

In this chapter, I should like to look at the place of communicative tasks within the broader framework of lessons or units of work. We shall look at a number of different ways in which tasks can be sequenced, and we shall also look at the integration of communicative tasks with other task and exercise types which are designed to help students develop the enabling skills they will need to communicate successfully, or which are designed to develop such skills as learning-how-to-learn.

Because the texts used to illustrate the points made in this chapter are, in some cases, rather lengthy, they are included as Appendix A, rather than being interpolated into the body of the chapter.

6.2 A psycholinguistic processing approach

Nunan (1985) suggests that activities can be graded according to the cognitive and performance demands made upon the learner. The following steps in a possible teaching sequence require the learner to undertake activities which make progressively more demands upon them, moving from comprehension based activities to controlled production activities, and finally ones which require the learner to engage in real communicative interaction:

A. *Processing* (comprehending)
   1. Read or listen to a text – no overt response.
   2. Read or listen to a text and give a non-verbal, physical response (e.g. learner raises hand every time key words are heard).
   3. Read or listen to a text and give a non-physical, non-verbal response (e.g. tick a box or grid each time key words are heard).
   4. Read or listen to a text and give a verbal response (repeat or write key words when they are heard).

B. *Productive*
   5. Listen to cue utterances, dialogue fragments and repeat.
   6. Listen to a cue and complete a substitution or transformation drill.

7. Listen to a cue (e.g. a question) and give a meaningful response (i.e. one that is true for the learner).

C. *Interactive*

8. Simulation (e.g. having listened to a conversation in which people talk about their family, students, working from role cards, circulate and find other members of their family).
9. Discussion (e.g. students in small groups talk about their own families).
10. Problem solving (e.g. in an information gap task, students are split into three groups; each group listens to an incomplete description of a family; students recombine and have to complete a family tree, identify which picture from a number of alternatives represents the family etc.).

In this ten-step sequence, the demands on the learners gradually increase. This sequence, which could be used as the basis for a unit of work, illustrates the notion of task continuity, where skills acquired or practised in one step are then utilised and extended in succeeding steps.

A sample lesson based on these steps is included as Extract 1 in Appendix A.

6.3 Task continuity

Task continuity refers to the chaining of activities together to form a sequence, in which the successful completion of prior activities is a prerequisite for succeeding ones. Under this principle, activities are sequenced, not only according to their complexity as determined by input, learner and activity factors, but also by the logic of themes and learning pathways.

The continuity principle has been used most successfully in the *Challenges* materials. In fact, in these materials, matters are complicated still further as teachers and learners can choose their own alternative pathways through the materials. The organisation of the activity chains in each learning module is described in the following way.

Thematically, the CHAINS in each Module each handle one aspect of the view taken of the Unit Theme by that Module. If there are five Chains, for example, in a Module, then learners will have the opportunity (if they want to) to work through five different ways of looking at that general view of the theme. But remember: there is no rule that says that all the Chains in a given Module have to be worked through.

Let us take an example from SOMETHING TO SAY, the Module titled: *WAYS*

119

Sequencing and integrating

TO SAY IT: There are *six* Chains in this Module, and, as a result, *six* aspects of the Module view of the theme:

A: Slanted information in the mass media. Sorting out facts from opinions.
B: The idea of a Community Newspaper: '*Lower Down*'.
C: How to get your opinions across in public: slogans & speeches.
D: How to find out what other people think about a problem: using question-naires.
How to get your opinion across in public: writing to newspapers.
E: Who do we talk to, and what do we talk about?
F: How to search for information. Using study skills to broaden your knowledge.

Hopefully, you can see how the Chains attack the theme in different ways, and how you might become involved in the theme through different *entry points*.
Organisationally and pedagogically, the Chains provide a framework for a series of skill *Steps* (*q.v.*) leading up to a more complex communicative activity, a *Task* (*q.v.*). Here is an example from Chain b of the 'first' Module in the Unit SOMEWHERE TO LIVE:

Step 1: Learners listen to a taped telephone conversation in which the line is bad and the participants constantly have to use language which shows that they have not heard correctly what the other person said. As a result, they often have to repeat what they said, and, in doing so, they express their message in a different way.
Step 2: Learners can do a True/False exercise to make sure that they have caught the gist of the conversation on the telephone.
Step 3: Learners can then do a listening and note-taking exercise in which they note down the ways in which the speakers showed they had not heard, and the ways in which they repeated what they had to say.
Task: Learners are then given a partial or 'defective' dialogue in the form of a telephone conversation of the same kind as they have experienced. Here they can make use of the expressions for '*showing you haven't heard*' and '*repeating things*' which they have noted down.

Candlin and Edelhoff: Challenges Teacher's Book, p. 26

Developing interlinked sets of activities in which succeeding steps are dependent on those which come before (either in terms of content or skills), will ensure greater coherence and consistency for your language programme.

Look at Extract 2 in Appendix A, which is taken from the *Challenges* coursebook. Here chains of tasks require the learner to undertake a variety of activities. Note the way in which the various macroskills are integrated and sequenced. Note as well the way in which tasks vary in their form/function focus. In 'chain a', for instance, the learner is required to engage in the following sequence of tasks:

120

STEP 1. READING The learner is first required to read a short passage which provides them with background information on one of the central characters and her search for accommodation.

STEP 2. QUESTIONNAIRE This task involves reading and writing. The learner is required to scan the text presented in Step 1 and extract specific information. In some cases, this requires the reader to make inferences. (For example, item 6 requires the reader to determine whether Charlotte would prefer to live in or out of London. There is no explicit statement about this in the text, and the reader must infer that because Charlotte prefers not to live with her parents, even though they live within commuting distance of the city, that she wants to live in London.)

STEP 3. WRITING This is a form-focused, gap-filling exercise in which learners are required to come up with the appropriate past tense form of a variety of regular and irregular verbs. In the process, they obtain additional information about Charlotte and her quest for a suitable place to live.

STEP 4. READING Learners read a series of 'to let' advertisements.

STEP 5. NOTE-TAKING In this step, learners are required to extract specific information from the advertisements and record this under a series of headings.

STEP 6. DISCUSSION This exercise is a form of meaningful drill in which learners are given controlled practice in giving reasons why they think a particular flat is or is not suitable for Charlotte.

Task 1:

This task is also a form of meaningful drill in which learners express their own preferences for one or other of the flats.

Task 2:

Finally, in a controlled writing task, learners are provided with model advertisements, and are required to write their own advertisement.

> In Extract 2, the first six activities are called 'chains' and the last two 'tasks'. What is the difference between the two?

It is rather difficult to see exactly how the authors differentiate between 'step' and 'task'. While activities 1–6 require learners to extract and manipulate information about Charlotte, the tasks require them to contribute personal information about themselves. However, such a distinction does not seem to be a particularly significant one. (It could also be argued that Step 6 also requires the learners to contribute something of themselves – in this instance, attitudinal rather than factual information.)

> Study the rest of Extract 2 and see whether you can find any other differences between 'steps' and 'tasks'. Does the remainder of the unit bear out the distinction I have drawn or not?

6.4 Information gap tasks

We have noted at various points the prominence of information gap tasks in communicative methodology. Unlike many other task and activity types, the use of such tasks has been supported by several pieces of classroom research. Information gaps can, in fact, act as a nucleus around which a range of other task and exercise types can be constructed.

This is exemplified in Appendix A Extract 3, where we see a unit which is built around an information gap task. The task contains the following steps.

1. *Introduction*
   Learners are introduced to the problem they will have to solve.
2. *Vocabulary and idioms*
   The teacher introduces vocabulary items which might cause difficulty.
3. *Small group listening, discussion and note taking*
   Students are divided into three groups. Each group is given a cassette tape and a set of questions. They are instructed to listen to the tape and answer the questions. The tape may be replayed as often as necessary.
4. *Small group problem solving*
   Students are recombined so that the new groups contain at least one member of each of the preceding groups. They are provided with a blank information table and an outline plan of a house. They must set out the key information in the information table, and then use this to construct a plan of the house.
5. *Feedback*
   Students return to their original groups and compare plans. They then compare their plans with the original which is provided by the teacher.

In this unit, all activities are designed around the problem-solving task, which occurs in Step 4. While most of the activities in a task of this sort are focused on extracting, recording and sharing information in various class groupings, it is also possible to interpose exercises which focus learners on various aspects of the linguistic code. In the example provided in the Appendix, only Step 2 focuses on language. However, it would be relatively easy to design other exercises to give learners practice in identifying and manipulating aspects of the linguistic system. While such exercises can occur either before or after the problem-solving activity, it is generally more desirable to introduce them after the problem has been solved. This is so the students' focus is not deflected from the central task in hand, and so they do not become bored with the problem-solving task itself. Another advantage is that students are reprocessing texts which they have already worked through at least once, and so, presumably, are reasonably familiar with them.

> Study Extract 3 and list several follow-up exercises
> which focus the learner on some aspect or aspects of the
> linguistic system.

There are any number of exercises which might be derived from one or more of the texts. Learners could be provided with written gapped versions of all or part of any of the texts and be required to reconstruct the original with or without access to the tape. In Text 1, students could be asked to identify the antecedents of the various anaphoric reference items. In Text 2 there are several noun phrases which are premodified with more than one adjective, for example 'lovely open fireplace', 'large grassed area'. Students could be asked to find these and then to rewrite a number of jumbled phrases so the adjectives occur in the correct order.

By deriving language exercises from the texts (rather than deciding on the grammatical points one wants to teach and constructing texts to exemplify these) one is able to present learners with more realistic texts. In any case, if one is using authentic materials, one must go from text to language rather than the other way round.

You will notice that, like the other tasks studied in this chapter, the information gap task presented here integrates all four macroskills. Learners must listen, make notes, discuss and report back. Admittedly, the major focus is on listening and speaking, but it would not be difficult to think of additional reading and writing activities if one wanted to. For example, paraphrased summaries of the texts could be given to the small groups to read and discuss as a preliminary to Step 3.

Another book which integrates skills and exploits the information gap principle is *Think Twice*. A unit from this book is included in Appendix A as Extract 4.

According to the author 'activities are communicative'. 'Communicative' is characterised as follows:

In each activity the student is given a task. Since the information they need for the task is split into two parts (Student A and Student B), no student has enough information to be able to do it alone. Accordingly, the students have to ask each other for the information they need and come to a decision together.

In this sense, the activities are not exercises, but contexts in which the students can use language to find out about things they genuinely need to know and to share ideas.

(Hover 1986a: 1)

> To what extent do you think the terms 'information gap' and 'communicative' should be synonymous? What are some of the other classroom tasks which can legitimately claim to be 'communicative'?

The following steps are recommended for the 'Housing Committee' unit.

1. Reading and writing: Students scan the letter on page 46 and complete the form at the bottom of the page.
2. Reading and thinking: Students read the advertisements on page 48 and decide which one to give Youn Hou.
3. Reading, listening and speaking: Students work in pairs. Student A looks at the information on page 45, Student B looks at the information on page 47. Student B must obtain information on Anne Littleton and Harry Marden from Student A, complete the housing request forms, and find them suitable accommodation from the advertisements on page 48.

> Each unit in the book practises a structure or function. Which language item or items is Unit 18 practising? Can you think of any pre- or post-task exercises for introducing or practising vocabulary, grammar or functions?
>
> Do you agree with Hover's claim that the activities are not exercises but contexts in which learners can use language to find out things they genuinely need to know? Where do you think that the unit might reside on the real-world/pedagogic continuum?
>
> Examine some of your own listening and reading texts. Can any of these be modified or adapted into an information gap task?

6.5 Content-based units

The use of experiential content as the basic building block in lesson or unit design is not a new one. As it has been around for a long time, it has many variants. Many of the courses and textbooks for English for Specific Purposes take as their point of departure content or topics from other subject areas. Another example of content-based courses are the foreign language 'immersion' programmes in which school students learn maths, science, history etc. through the target language. (In a sense, as language is used as a vehicle to talk about other things, all language classes have a content dimension.)

A topic approach to ESL in a school setting has been developed by Evans (1986). Topics are broken into four sequential stages.

STAGE 1: VISUAL PRESENTATION

In the first stage, central concepts are presented through pictures, maps, models etc. Appropriate structures and vocabulary are introduced, and students are given the opportunity of describing what they have seen orally and in writing.

STAGE 2: BUILDING A READING PASSAGE

Students answer true/false questions about the visuals and use these as the basis for building a written passage.

STAGE 3: ANALYSING AND EXTENDING THE READING PASSAGE

At this stage, students focus on some of the linguistic elements in the passage.

STAGE 4: CREATING A PASSAGE

In the final stage, students produce their own written passage based on the language and content they have acquired in Stages 1–3. The point of departure may be another visual which might be described or compared with the original visual.

The Topic Framework

Teacher Input ——————— ‐ ‐ ‐ ‐ ‐ ‐ Student Input

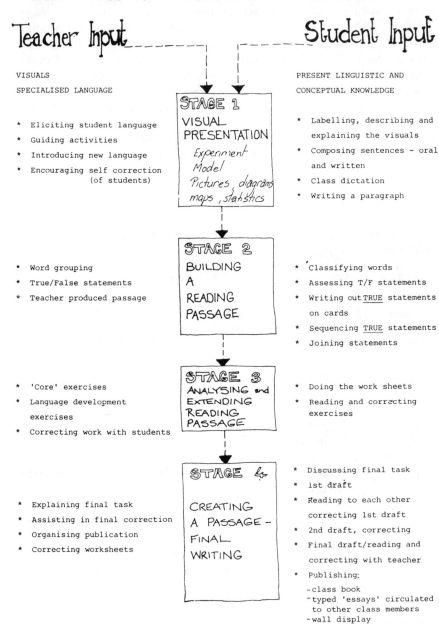

VISUALS

SPECIALISED LANGUAGE

* Eliciting student language
* Guiding activities
* Introducing new language
* Encouraging self correction
  (of students)

STAGE 1
VISUAL PRESENTATION
Experiment
Model
Pictures, diagrams,
maps, statistics

PRESENT LINGUISTIC AND

CONCEPTUAL KNOWLEDGE

* Labelling, describing and
  explaining the visuals
* Composing sentences - oral
  and written
* Class dictation
* Writing a paragraph

---

* Word grouping
* True/False statements
* Teacher produced passage

STAGE 2
BUILDING A READING PASSAGE

* Classifying words
* Assessing T/F statements
* Writing out TRUE statements
  on cards
* Sequencing TRUE statements
* Joining statements

---

* 'Core' exercises
* Language development
  exercises
* Correcting work with students

STAGE 3
ANALYSING and EXTENDING READING PASSAGE

* Doing the work sheets
* Reading and correcting
  exercises

---

* Explaining final task
* Assisting in final correction
* Organising publication
* Correcting worksheets

STAGE 4
CREATING A PASSAGE - FINAL WRITING

* Discussing final task
* 1st draft
* Reading to each other
  correcting 1st draft
* 2nd draft, correcting
* Final draft/reading and
  correcting with teacher
* Publishing:
  - class book
  - typed 'essays' circulated
    to other class members
  - wall display

Evans: Learning English through Content Areas, p. 7

126

Like the other approaches we have looked at in this chapter, the topic approach integrates the four macroskills. The framework gradually extends the demands made on the learners until they reach the point where they are able to produce their own original piece of writing.

Although the particular variant of content-based teaching described here is for ESL learners in secondary schools, it has also been adapted to other situations and contexts. These include EFL and adult ESL. You might like to consider the extent to which a content or topic-based approach could work in your own teaching situation.

A slightly different, although not totally unrelated approach, is adopted by Hamp-Lyons and Heasley (1987). The units in their book on the development of writing skills are based on what might be called rhetorical macrofunctions such as classifying, defining, generalising, comparing and contrasting, etc.

The first unit from their book is included as Extract 5 in Appendix A. The structure of the unit is summarised below. You will notice that many of the tasks involve only a minimal amount of writing. As you look at each task, try and determine what they are intended to achieve, i.e. ask yourself why the authors have created this particular task.

Task 1 *Read and discuss*
Students read a short text and study an accompanying visual. They then discuss with their partner the extent to which the visual facilitates comprehension of the text.

Task 2 *Read, note and discuss*
Students read a short text and carry out several activities including creating a visual to accompany the text.

Task 3 *Write*
Students study a picture, make a list of prepositions of place, and use these in writing four descriptive sentences.

Task 4 *Read and discuss*
Students read a text, draw an accompanying visual and discuss the text with a partner.

Task 5 *Read and discuss*
Students read a text, create a visual to accompany it and compare this with one created by another student.

Task 6 *Read and draw*
Students read a text and produce an accompanying visual.

Task 7 *Read and think*
Students read a text, study an accompanying visual and decide whether or not the visual aid facilitates comprehension of the text.

Task 8 *Read and think*
Students compare two short texts and decide which is easier to understand.

127

Task   9 *Read and find*
    Students scan a text and find locational expressions.
Task 10 *Read and draw*
    Students reread the text from Task 9, identify its organising principle and create a visual.
Task 11 *Read and relate*
    Students read a text, relate parts of an accompanying visual to information in the text.

The unit concludes with three consolidation tasks in which students study various visuals and write short texts based on these.

As you can see, it is only when students reach the end of the unit that they are required to write texts themselves. The bulk of the unit is devoted to tasks which exemplify and model ways of describing spatial relationships.

> Study the unit and decide on the extent to which it exemplifies the 'task continuity' principle. In other words, are the tasks satisfactorily interrelated or not? (One way of determining whether tasks are interdependent or not is to change their sequencing. If, for example, Tasks 6, 7, and 8 can be swapped for Tasks 2, 3, and 4, then the tasks are obviously not 'dependent' in the same sense as those in Extract 1.)

6.6 Interactive problem solving

In this section, we shall look at two approaches in which communicative tasks are sequenced around problem situations. The first is Scarcella's sociodrama, while the second is Di Pietro's strategic interaction. Both approaches allow the teacher to build in exercises which enable learners to develop vocabulary, grammar and discourse as well as interactive skills.

The focus of Scarcella's sociodrama is on the development of skills in social interaction. Unlike most role plays, sociodrama involves a series of specific steps. It is student- rather than teacher-centred in that students define their own roles and determine their own course of action. The following set of steps provides an idea of how the approach works.

1. *Warm up*
   The topic is introduced by the teacher.
2. *Presentation of new vocabulary*
   New words and expressions are introduced.

3. *Presentation of dilemma*
   A story is introduced by the teacher who stops at the dilemma point. Students focus on the conflict which occurs at the dilemma point.
4. *Discussion of the situation and selection of roles*
   The problem and roles are discussed. Students who relate to the roles and who have solutions to offer come to the front of the class to participate in the enactment.
5. *Audience preparation*
   Those who are not going to take part in the enactment are given specific tasks to carry out during the enactment.
6. *Enactment*
   Role-players act out the solution which has been suggested.
7. *Discussion of the situation and selection of new role-players*
   Alternative ways of solving the problem are explored and new role-players are selected.
8. *Re-enactment*
   The problem situation is replayed with new strategies.
9. *Summary*
   The teacher guides the students to summarise what was presented.
10. *Follow-up*
    These may include a written exercise, extended discussion, aural comprehension exercises or a reading exercise.

(Scarcella 1978)

Di Pietro's approach, which he calls 'strategic interaction' is based on improvisations or 'scenarios'. Students act out scenarios, having first memorised the situation and roles they are expected to play and having carefully rehearsed the scenario. However, at certain points during the acting out, additional information is injected into the situation, requiring learners to modify their intended role, and to alter the direction of the interaction.

> Do you think these approaches might have a pedagogic or real-world rationale?

With a little thought, problem situations and scenarios can be developed which do allow learners to rehearse 'real-world' language i.e. language they might potentially need to use in the real world. Whether or not a given lesson appears to have a real-world rationale really depends on the situation which the teacher has chosen. Scarcella obviously believes that her approach has real-world applications as can be seen in the following quote:

Socio-drama is an activity which obliges students to attend to the verbal environment. First, it is relevant to the students' interests, utilizing both extrinsic motivation, which refers to the students' daily interests and cares, and intrinsic motivation, which refers to the students' internal feelings and attitudes. . . . Furthermore, socio-drama is a problem-solving activity which stimulates real life situations and requires active student involvement.

(Scarcella 1978: 46)

> What principles seem to underlie the sequencing of activities in these two problem-based approaches?

6.7 The integrated language lesson

In this final section we shall look at a way of incorporating a range of desirable characteristics into a communicative lesson format. The section is based on a unit which systematically attempts to incorporate a range of factors hypothesised to facilitate language learning. This is included as Extract 6 in Appendix A.

The aim of the unit is to provide learners with the opportunity of practising language associated with going to a restaurant. The following principles were drawn on by the authors in developing the unit. The rationale for most of these criteria can be found in the discussions in Part I.

1. *Authenticity*
   The taped conversation which provides the point of departure for the unit is scripted from authentic interactions between a waiter and restaurant customers.
2. *Task continuity*
   Activities in the unit build on those which go before. The language is progressively restructured as learners move from global, comprehension-based activities to those involving language production and analysis.
3. *Real-world focus*
   The unit makes explicit the link between the classroom and the real world by a) allowing the in-class rehearsal of real-world tasks, and b) setting learners out-of-class assignments and tasks.
4. *Language focus*
   Based on the belief that adolescent and adult learners can benefit from a systematic exposure to the language system, the unit contains activities which focus the learner on language. The activities are

designed on discovery learning principles, and learners are encouraged to identify patterns and regularities through discovery learning.

5. *Learning focus*

The unit also draws on recent work which suggests that the development of learning skills and skills in learning-how-to-learn are important for adult learners. In these activities, learners are encouraged to monitor themselves as learners, develop a range of learning strategies which seem to suit them best and develop skills in self-monitoring and self-evaluation.

6. *Language practice*

The unit contains an activity which provides learners with the opportunity for controlled oral practice in a communicative context.

7. *Problem solving*

Communicative problem-solving tasks which learners undertake in small groups can facilitate language acquisition.

Examine a unit of work from your own teaching programme or a coursebook you are currently using and summarise the principles on which it seems to be based. What are the similarities and differences between your list and the ones provided in this section?

This final extract demonstrates the way in which communicative tasks can be integrated with other exercise types in the development of lessons or units of work.

6.8 Conclusion

In this chapter we have looked at some of the ways in which communicative tasks can be sequenced and interrelated with other exercise and activity types.

Although the range of proposals set out here is by no means exhaustive, it does demonstrate the wide variety of ways in which communicative language tasks can be sequenced and integrated with other exercise types in language programmes. It also serves to exemplify a number of key principles which have been developed in preceding chapters.

One factor which has perhaps not been given the prominence it deserves is the role of the learner in sequencing tasks. The *Challenges* material alone invites learners to negotiate and establish their own learning sequences.

In conclusion, it may be useful to offer a set of criteria for evaluating the 'good' language lesson, and which may serve to guide the selection and sequencing of tasks and activities within such a lesson (see also Candlin 1987).

The 'good communicative language' lesson will:

- derive input from authentic sources
- involve learners in problem-solving activities in which they are required to negotiate meaning
- incorporate tasks which relate to learners' real-life communicative needs
- allow learners choices in what, how and when to learn
- allow learners to rehearse, in class, real-world language tasks
- require learners and teachers to adopt a range of roles, and use language in a variety of settings in and out of the classroom
- expose learners to the language as system
- encourage learners to develop skills in learning how to learn
- integrate the four macroskills
- provide controlled practice in enabling microskills
- involve learners in creative language use.

References and further reading

Abbs, B., C. Candlin, C. Edelhoff, T. Moston, and M. Sexton. 1978. *Challenges: Students' Book*. London: Longman.

Candlin, C. 1987. Towards task-based language learning. In C. Candlin and D. Murphy (Eds.) *Language Learning Tasks*. Englewood Cliffs NJ: Prentice-Hall.

Candlin, C., and C. Edelhoff. 1982. *Challenges: Teacher's Book*. London: Longman.

Di Pietro, R. 1987. *Strategic Interaction*. Cambridge: Cambridge University Press.

Evans, R. 1986. *Learning English Through Content Areas: The Topic Approach to ESL*. Melbourne: Ministry of Education.

Hamp-Lyons, L., and B. Heasley. 1987. *Study Writing*. Cambridge: Cambridge University Press.

Hover, D. 1986a. *Think Twice: Teacher's Book*. Cambridge: Cambridge University Press.

Hover, D. 1986b. *Think Twice: Students' Book*. Cambridge: Cambridge University Press.

Nunan, D. 1982. *What Do You Think?* Adelaide: Language Press.

Nunan, D. 1985. *Language Teaching Course Design: Trends and Issues*. Adelaide: National Curriculum Resource Centre.

Nunan, D. 1988. *Syllabus Design*. Oxford: Oxford University Press.

Scarcella, R. 1978. Socio-drama for social interaction. *TESOL Quarterly*, 12, 41–6.

7 Tasks and teacher development

7.1 Introduction: the self-directed teacher

In this the last chapter in the book, we shall look at some of the ways in which the ideas outlined in the preceding chapter might be applied. In particular, I would like to outline ways in which tasks may be designed and evaluated. I shall also describe a workshop procedure for introducing tasks. I suggest that 'task' can be viewed as 'content', and also as 'method', that is, as one of the means by which teacher education can be effected.

An important trend in language teacher development in recent years has been a move away from the teacher as passive recipient and implementer of other people's syllabuses and methods, towards the idea of the teacher as an active creator of his or her own materials, classroom activities and so on. Even in systems which have clearly articulated syllabuses and curriculum guidelines, there is scope for teachers to adapt and modify the syllabuses and materials with which they work. A major aspect of this present book, with its points for reflection and analysis, has been to encourage a more self-directed approach on the part of teachers.

Related to the notion of the self-directed teacher has been a break with the 'method' concept. For many years language teaching has been at the mercy of a number of competing methods. Some of these, such as Suggestopedia, the Silent Way and Community Language Learning, have been rather exotic, others, such as audiolingualism, have been more conservative. (For a comprehensive analysis of a range of more prominent methods, see Richards and Rodgers 1986.)

Despite their diversity, these competing methods have a number of things in common. One of these is the belief that somewhere is the 'one best method', that is, the method which will work for every conceivable learner in every conceivable context and learning situation. The methods also claim legitimacy in terms of psycholinguistic and psychological learning theory and practice. Thus audiolingualism drew its theoretical rationale from behaviourism, the Total Physical Response was based on selective 'findings' from first language acquisition, and Community Language Learning drew on certain tenets of humanistic psychology.

Richards (1987b) points out that the 'methods' all share something else:

> ... common to all of them is a set of prescriptions as to what
> teachers and learners should do in the language classroom. There
> are prescriptions for the teacher as to what material should be
> presented, when it should be taught and how, and prescriptions for
> learners as to what approach they should take towards the
> teaching materials and classroom activities.
>
> (Richards 1987b: 12)

Rather than importing ideas from elsewhere, I suggest that it is preferable
to identify what works and what does not work through the direct study
of the classroom itself. As it is teachers who are the crucial variable in the
teaching situation, it is important that teachers should study what goes
on in their own classroom. Self-analysis and evaluation will certainly be
characteristics of the self-directed teacher.

In Chapter 1 we saw that the concept of 'task' seemed to be a
particularly real one for teachers. In their major study of teachers at
work, Swaffar *et al.* (1982) found that teachers tended to plan their work
around tasks rather than methods. They concluded that:

> Methodological labels assigned to teaching activities are, in
> themselves, not informative, because they refer to a pool of
> classroom practices which are universally used. The differences
> among major methodologies are to be found in the ordered
> hierarchy, the priorities assigned to tasks. Not *what* classroom
> activity is used, but *when* and *how* form the the crux of the matter
> in distinguishing methodological practice.
>
> (Swaffar *et al.* 1982: 31)

In general education, Shavelson and Stern come to the conclusion, that:

> Most teachers are trained to plan instruction by (a) specifying
> (behavioural) objectives, (b) specifying students' entry behaviour,
> (c) selecting and sequencing learning behaviours so as to move
> learners from entry behaviours to objectives and (d) evaluating the
> outcomes of instruction in order to improve planning. While this
> prescriptive model of planning may be one of the most consistently
> taught features of the curriculum of teacher education programs,
> the model is consistently not used in teachers' planning in schools.
>
> (Shavelson and Stern 1981: 477)

This mismatch between what teachers are taught to do and what they
actually do arises, according to Shavelson and Stern, because once inside
the classroom the teacher must come up with a constant flow of activities
or face behavioural problems. Activities (or, as I have called them, tasks)
rather than the prescriptive ends-means model are the major focus of the
teacher's planning efforts.

In this chapter, we shall look at some of the ways in which teachers might be encouraged to think more systematically about tasks, and also at how tasks might be used as the basis for teacher development programmes. In section 7.4, I shall describe a workshop which was designed to get teachers thinking critically about the tasks they use.

7.2 Evaluating tasks

One of the most obvious ways of applying the information presented in the preceding chapters is in task evaluation. This involves adopting a more critical attitude towards classroom tasks that form the basis for one's teaching programme.

In his paper on task design, Candlin (1987) suggests that task evaluation should cover three broad areas. These are 'problematicity', 'implementability' and 'combinability'. Under the rubric of 'problematicity' one would consider the extent to which a given task reveals variations in learners' abilities and knowledge, the extent to which it is diagnostic or explanatory, whether it provides monitoring and feedback, and whether it can be used as a basis for future action. 'Implementability' leads one to a consideration of the resources required, the organisational and management complexity, and the adaptability of the task. Finally, 'combinability' requires us to consider the extent to which the task can be sequenced and integrated with other tasks.

While there will inevitably be an overlap between different evaluative criteria, I should like to propose the set of evaluative questions set out in the accompanying checklist. These reflect the various issues and concepts already covered in the six preceding chapters. The list of questions can be used in a variety of ways. You will not necessarily need or want to answer all questions in task evaluation. I would suggest that at particular times (when, for example, you are trying out a new task for the first time, or using a task which is familiar to you but not to your students) that you record the lesson in which the task is introduced on audio or videotape and use this to aid your reflection as you evaluate the task. An alternative would be to invite a colleague to observe your class and complete the evaluation for you.

CHECKLIST FOR EVALUATING COMMUNICATIVE TASKS

Goals and rationale
- To what extent is the goal or goals of the task obvious a) to you b) to your students?
- Is the task appropriate to the learners' proficiency level?
- To what extent does the task reflect a real-world or pedagogic rationale? Is this appropriate?

Teacher development

- Does the task encourage learners to apply classroom learning to the real world?
- What beliefs about the nature of language and learning are inherent in the task?
- Is the task likely to be interesting and motivating to the students?

Input
- What form does the input take?
- Is it authentic?
- If not, is it appropriate to the goal of the task?

Activities
- Are the activities appropriate to the communicative goals of the task?
- If not, can they be modified to make them more appropriate?
- Is the task designed to stimulate students to use bottom-up or top-down processing skills?
- Is there an information gap or problem which might prompt a negotiation of meaning?
- Are the activities appropriate to the input data?
- Are the activities designed in a way which will allow learners to communicate and cooperate in groups?

Roles and settings
- What learner and teacher roles are inherent in the task?
- Are they appropriate?
- What levels of complexity are there in the classroom organisation implicit in the task?
- Is the setting confined to the classroom?

Implementation
- Does the task actually engage the learners' interests?
- Do the activities prompt genuine communicative interaction among students?
- To what extent are learners encouraged to negotiate meaning?
- Does anything unexpected occur as the task is being carried out?
- What type of language is actually stimulated by the task?
- Is this different from what might have been predicted?

Grading and integration
- Is the task at the appropriate level of difficulty for the students?
- If not, is there any way in which the task might be modified in order to make it either easier or more challenging?
- Is the task so structured that it can be undertaken at different levels of difficulty?
- What are the principles upon which the tasks are sequenced?

- Do tasks exhibit the 'task continuity' principle?
- Are a range of macroskills integrated into the sequence of tasks?
- If not, can you think of ways in which they might be integrated?
- At the level of the unit or lesson, are communicative tasks integrated with other activities and exercises designed to provide learners with mastery of the linguistic system?
- If not, are there ways in which such activities might be introduced?
- Do the tasks incorporate exercises in learning-how-to-learn?
- If not, are there ways in which such exercises might be introduced?

Assessment and evaluation
- What means exist for the teacher to determine how successfully the learners have performed?
- Does the task have built into it some means whereby learners might judge how well they had performed?
- Is the task realistic in terms of the resources and teacher-expertise it demands?

7.3 Creating tasks

In addition to its use as a tool for evaluating tasks created by others, the checklist can also be used to guide you in developing your own tasks.

As we have already seen, the starting point for task design should be the goals and objectives which are set out in the syllabus or curriculum guidelines which underpin your teaching programme. You may need to augment or modify these if they are not written in a form which can be directly translated into communicative tasks. Objectives may, for instance, be set out as checklists of grammatical items such as the following:

> At the end of the course learners will be able to use the present continuous tense to describe actions in progress.

Most syllabuses and curriculum guidelines will provide some sort of rationale. This may be a broad statement of intent, such as:

> The course should develop reading and writing skills for tertiary study, *or*
> The focus will be on the survival skills needed by learners in the target culture.

Even these very general statements provide a point of departure for task design.

The next step is selecting or creating input for learners to work with. In the preceding chapters, we have seen that the use of authentic input is a central characteristic of communicative tasks. You will need to consider whether or not it is possible for you to use authentic data. Your decision will depend on such factors as the attitude of your learners and the availability of resources. Many low-level learners are traumatised when first exposed to authentic samples of language, and have to be taught that it is not necessary to understand every word for communication to be successful. Teachers working in a foreign language context will be faced with greater difficulty in obtaining authentic samples of input than second language teachers, particularly in obtaining aural input data.

Where possible, it is desirable to build up a 'bank' of data. These can be classified and filed under topics or themes, and provide a ready-made resource to be drawn on when designing tasks. As indicated earlier, one should work from the data to the teaching/learning objectives, rather than the other way round. In other words, it is better to derive communicative activities and other exercises, such as grammatical manipulation exercises, from the input, rather than, say, deciding to teach a particular item, and then creating a text to exemplify the target feature or item.

When designing activities, you need to decide whether you want learners to rehearse in class tasks which they will, potentially at least, want to carry out in the real world. If the tasks have a pedagogic rationale, you need to be clear what this is. It is not good enough to set learners tasks on the basis that they seemed a good idea at the time, or because they worked well with another class. You also need to consider the roles that both you and the learners will adopt in carrying out the task and assess whether these roles are appropriate to the given group. Settings and learner configurations also need to be considered. Getting learners in and out of groups of different sizes quickly and efficiently so that time on task is maximised is an important classroom management skill.

When monitoring the task, you will want to keep a close check on the actual language which is generated. This will often differ from what had been predicted. It is a good idea to record teacher-fronted and small group interactions from time to time and use these to review and evaluate the task.

7.4 An in-service workshop

In this section, I should like to outline a procedure for introducing teachers to the notion of 'task' as a basic tool for programme planning and evaluation. The case study presented here is designed to demonstrate what task-focused teacher education looks like.

The workshop was originally devised as the first in a series on language curriculum design. The concept of 'task' was selected for the initial workshop as experience has shown that it is the one curriculum element which is most familiar and accessible to classroom teachers. (As we have seen, this is also the conclusion reached by Shavelson and Stern 1981.) In addition, as Candlin and Murphy (1987) have pointed out, tasks embody a curriculum in miniature. It was therefore felt that a workshop on tasks would provide a 'user-friendly' introduction to wider curriculum issues.

Step 1:   Pre-workshop task

Teachers are asked several weeks in advance to provide a detailed description of a task which works particularly well for them. They are asked to provide information on the target audience for the task, the goal(s), activities, learner roles and groupings.

Step 2:   The 'good' language learning task

The first workshop activity is designed to get participants to identify those characteristics which they feel the 'good' language task should possess. To this end, they are asked to rate a series of statements from 0 to 4 according to whether these statements were characteristic of the 'good' task. The statements were taken from a variety of sources (some of which you will recognise from preceding chapters) and are set out below.

QUESTIONNAIRE ON THE 'GOOD' LEARNING TASK

What do you believe?
Circle the appropriate number following each of the criteria below according to the following scale:
0 – this is not a characteristic of a good task
1 – this characteristic may be present, but is optional
2 – this characteristic is reasonably important
3 – this characteristic is extremely important
4 – this characteristic is essential

Good learning tasks should:
1. enable learners to manipulate and practise specific
   features of language   0/1/2/3/4

2. allow learners to rehearse, in class, communicative skills
   they will need in the real world   0/1/2/3/4

3. activate psychological/psycholinguistic processes of
   learning   0/1/2/3/4

4. be suitable for mixed ability groups   0/1/2/3/4

5. involve learners in solving a problem, coming to a conclusion	0/1/2/3/4
6. be based on authentic or naturalistic source material	0/1/2/3/4
7. involve learners in sharing information	0/1/2/3/4
8. require the use of more than one macroskill	0/1/2/3/4
9. allow learners to think and talk about language and learning	0/1/2/3/4
10. promote skills in learning how to learn	0/1/2/3/4
11. have clear objectives stating what learners will be able to do as a result of taking part in the task	0/1/2/3/4
12. utilise the community as a resource	0/1/2/3/4
13. give learners a choice in what they do and the order in which they do it	0/1/2/3/4
14. involve learners in risk-taking	0/1/2/3/4
15. require learners to rehearse, rewrite and polish initial efforts	0/1/2/3/4
16. enable learners to share in the planning and development of the task	0/1/2/3/4
17. have built into them a means of evaluating the success or otherwise of the task	0/1/2/3/4

Step 3: Selecting essential characteristics

Having completed the questionnaire on their own, participants then work in pairs to select the five characteristics which they consider to be essential to a good task. This step involves considerable negotiation for those participants who disagree with their partner (and there is usually some disagreement amongst most groups). When disagreements arise, participants are asked to consider why they disagree, to provide evidence for their views, and to identify whether this evidence is based on fact, experience or opinion.

Step 4: Task analysis

Once participants have established their criteria, they are given copies of the tasks sent in prior to the workshop. These are presented in a way which makes it impossible for the authors to be identified. They are asked to rate each task from 0 to 3 according to the extent to which they embody the criteria of a good task which the participants themselves have nominated. The scale they are asked to use is as follows:

0 this feature is not reflected in the task at all
1 this feature is slightly reflected in the task
2 this feature is given quite a lot of prominence in the task
3 this feature is given a great deal of prominence in the task.

This step has to be handled with some care. The principal aim of the exercise is not to criticise the tasks but to encourage participants to evaluate the criteria they have selected against the sorts of tasks they had originally provided. At the end of the workshop, participants very often state that they have given low ratings to their own tasks, and that the exercise has prompted them to review their approach to task selection.

Step 5: Criteria for determining task difficulty

Step 5 is devoted to the issue of task difficulty. The following sets of criteria, from a variety of sources, are provided to participants who want to use them. They are asked to talk through these and come up with their own list of criteria for determining task difficulty.

FACTORS TO BE TAKEN INTO CONSIDERATION IN DETERMINING TASK DIFFICULTY

Brindley (1987): learner, task and text factors will interact to determine task difficulty.

Easier ——————————————→More difficult

Learner

is confident about task	is not confident
is motivated to carry out task	is not motivated
has necessary prior learning experiences	no prior experiences
can learn at pace required	cannot learn at required pace
has necessary language skills	does not have language skills
has relevant cultural knowledge	no relevant cultural knowledge

Task

low cognitive complexity	cognitively complex
has few steps	has many steps
plenty of context provided	no context
plenty of help available	no help available
does not require grammatical accuracy	grammatical accuracy required
has as much time as necessary	has little time

Text

is short, not dense (few facts)	is long and dense (many facts)
clear presentation	presentation not clear
plenty of contextual clues	few contextual clues
familiar, everyday content	unfamiliar content

Brown and Yule (1983): factors related to the speaker, listener, content, support and purpose will affect task difficulty.

Easier ——————————————→More difficult

one speaker	many speakers
interesting/involving	boring/non-involving
simple syntax	complex syntax
specific vocabulary	generalised vocabulary
familiar content	unfamiliar content
narratives/instructions	argument/explanation/opinion
temporal sequence	non-temporal sequence
contextual support	no contextual support
visual aids present	visual aids absent
learner involved as a participant	learner as observer

Nunan (1985): difficulty determined by type of learner response.

Easier

Comprehension
  Listen/read, no response
  Listen/read, non-verbal response
  Listen/read, verbal response
Production
  Listen/read and repeat/copy
  Listen/read, carry out drill
  Listen/read, respond meaningfully
Interaction
  Listen/read, rehearse
  Listen/read, role play
  Listen/read, solve problem/come to conclusion

More difficult

Anderson and Lynch (1988): difficulty determined by information sequence, topic familiarity, explicitness, non-verbal support and item correspondence.

Easier ——————————————→More difficult

information presented in sequence	information out of sequence

topic is familiar	topic is unfamiliar
topic is familiar	topic is unfamiliar
information is explicit	information requires inferences
graphic/non-verbal support present	graphic support absent
item correspondence	

blank $\rightarrow$ repetition $\rightarrow$ synonym $\rightarrow$ compatible $\rightarrow$ ambiguous $\rightarrow$ contradictory

---

Step 6: Applying difficulty criteria

In the final step, participants are given sets of sample tasks and are asked to rank these from the easiest to the most difficult according to the criteria they selected in Step 5.

> At this point, you might like to select a task which you feel works particularly well for you and work through the various steps outlined above.

7.5 Conclusion

In this final chapter, I have tried to broaden the focus a little to show how the concept of task can be introduced and related to teaching practice. In the process, I have also tried to show how tasks can be used as a vehicle for introducing concepts related to the broader field of curriculum study. They can also be used as a point of departure for small-scale classroom research projects by teachers themselves. Such projects should lead teachers to see the relevance of theory for the practical concerns of the classroom.

Postscript

I began this book by considering two views of language teaching, and so it is fitting that I should conclude by returning to the points I made earlier.

In language teaching, as in general education, there has been a move away from a top-down approach to the planning, implementation and evaluation of teaching programmes. The top-down approach is characterised by curriculum plans, syllabus outlines and methodological procedures which are designed by 'experts' and delivered as a package to the classroom practitioner. In-service and professional development programmes are principally designed to train teachers how to use these

143

externally developed syllabuses, materials and methods. In language teaching, the top-down approach resulted in a spate of methods developed during the sixties and early seventies. Alongside audiolingualism and cognitive code learning, there were the more exotic methods such as Total Physical Response (Asher 1977), Community Language Learning (Curran 1976), Suggestopedia (the most accessible introduction to the principles of Suggestopedia is Ostrander and Schroeder 1981) and, more recently, the 'Natural' Approach (Krashen and Terrell 1983). These methods are described and criticised in Richards and Rodgers (1986). (A table summarising these various approaches and derived from Richards and Rodgers is included as Appendix B.) Most of these methods have one thing in common: they assume that there is one best way of learning a second or foreign language, and they provide a set of principles and procedures, which, it is believed, if followed properly by the classroom practitioner, will result in learning.

With the recent break from the 'method' concept has come the development of more bottom-up approaches to language teaching. The curriculum is being rediscovered, not as a set of prescriptive edicts, but as the documentation and systematisation of classroom practice (Nunan 1988a). Curriculum designers are becoming concerned with identifying principles of effective teaching from within the classroom itself. This is reflected in the current interest in classroom-oriented research (see, for example, Seliger and Long 1983; Chaudron 1988; van Lier 1988).

Another theme which has been reiterated in various guises in recent years is the need in pre- and in-service teacher education programmes for a balance between theory and practice. It is also important for participants to appreciate the complementary nature of theory and practice. This is unlikely to be achieved in teacher education programmes in which the theoretical and practical components are kept apart. Bottom-up and classroom-oriented approaches to curriculum development, on the other hand, are particularly amenable to achieving an appropriate balance between theory and practice.

A major trend in language teaching in recent years has been the adoption of learner-centred approaches to curriculum development. Learner-centred approaches are characterised by the involvement of the learner, and the utilisation of information about the learner in all aspects of the curriculum process (Nunan 1988a: 6).

Brundage and MacKeracher (1980) and Knowles (1983) argue for a client-centred approach to adult learning on the grounds that adults value their own experience as a resource for further learning, and that they learn best when they have a personal investment in the programme and when the content is personally relevant.

Given the trends and issues which I have just referred to, I would like to propose the following principles for teacher development programmes, particularly post-experience or in-service programmes. Here, teachers are looking for guidance in solving problems which confront them in the classroom. Therefore, there must be explicit links between the content of professional development programmes and the classroom.

1. Content and methodology should be perceived as being personally relevant;
2. theory should be derived from practice;
3. the approach should be bottom-up rather than top-down;
4. teachers should be involved in the structuring of the professional development programme;
5. content should, as far as possible, be derived from the teachers themselves;
6. desirable practice should be modelled in the professional development programme;

and last but not least, given the focus of this book

7. because they are particularly salient for teachers, and also because they provide a convenient point of entry into other areas of curriculum planning, implementation and evaluation, tasks should be given a prominent place in pre- and in-service professional development programmes designed to introduce participants to principles of curriculum design and development.

One of the most effective ways of incorporating these principles into teacher development programmes is to use input from teachers themselves. We have seen one way in which this might work, although there are many other variants. For example, one might give all workshop participants some input several weeks in advance of the workshop and ask them to a) create a task based on the input; b) get their students to undertake the task; c) record them as they do so. The workshop would then consist of participants describing their tasks along the lines already suggested (i.e. in terms of goals, input, activities, learner and teacher roles and evaluation). Following this, they could look at similarities and differences and make suggestions as to how and why these came about. The coordinator could then bring the workshop to a conclusion with a summary of theory and principles underlying the discussions.

Extending the principle of teacher input forming the basis of professional development workshops, it is usually possible to get teachers to identify some issue, problem or question which they would like to follow up. Teachers would set up a small-scale investigation in their classroom and report back to the workshop group at a later date. In this way, teachers can be encouraged to adopt an action research orientation to their work. Such an orientation allows theory to be integrated with practice.

Teacher development

References and further reading

Anderson, A., and T. Lynch. 1988. *Listening*. Oxford: Oxford University Press.
Asher, J. 1977. *Learning Another Language Through Actions: The Complete Teacher's Guide Book*. Los Gatos Calif.: Sky Oaks Productions.
Brindley, G. 1987. Factors affecting task difficulty. In D. Nunan *Guidelines for the Development of Curriculum Resources for the Adult Migrant Education Program*. Adelaide: National Curriculum Resource Centre.
Brown, G., and G. Yule. 1983. *Teaching the Spoken Language*. Cambridge: Cambridge University Press.
Brundage, D. H., and MacKeracher, D. 1980. *Adult Learning Principles and Their Application to Program Planning*. Ontario: Ontario Institute for Studies in Education.
Candlin, C. 1987. Towards task-based language learning. In C. Candlin and D. Murphy (Eds.).
Candlin, C., and D. Murphy (Eds.). 1987. *Language Learning Tasks*. Englewood Cliffs, N.J.: Prentice-Hall International.
Chaudron, C. 1988. *Second Language Classrooms: Research on Teaching and Learning*. Cambridge: Cambridge University Press.
Curran, C. 1976. *Counselling-Learning in Second Languages*. Apple River Ill.: Apple River Press.
Knowles, M. 1983. *The Adult Learner: A Neglected Species*. Houston: Gulf Publishing Company.
Krashen, S., and T. Terrell. 1983. *The Natural Approach*. Oxford: Pergamon Press.
van Lier, L. 1988. *The Classroom and the Language Learner: Ethnography and Second-Language Classroom Research*. London: Longman.
Nunan, D. 1985. *Language Teaching Course Design: Trends and Issues*. Adelaide: National Curriculum Resource Centre.
Nunan, D. 1988a. *The Learner-Centred Curriculum*. Cambridge: Cambridge University Press.
Nunan, D. 1988b. *Syllabus Design*. Oxford: Oxford University Press.
Ostrander, S., and L. Schroeder. 1981. *Superlearning*. London: Sphere Books.
Ramani, E. 1987. Theorizing from the classroom. *English Language Teaching Journal*, 41 (1), 3–11.
Richards, J. 1987b. Beyond methods: alternative approaches to instructional design in language teaching. *Prospect*, 3 (1), 11–30.
Richards, J., and T. Rodgers. 1986. *Approaches and Methods in Language Teaching*. Cambridge: Cambridge University Press.
Seliger, H., and M. Long. 1983. *Classroom-Oriented Research*. Rowley Mass.: Newbury House.
Shavelson, R. J., and P. Stern. 1981. Research on teachers' pedagogical thoughts, judgements, decisions and behaviour. *Review of Educational Research*, 51, 4.
Swaffar, J., K. Arens, and M. Morgan. 1982. Teacher classroom practices: redefining method as task hierarchy. *Modern Language Journal*, 66, 1.

Appendix A A selection of tasks and units of work

The materials in Appendix A have been extracted from the following sources:

EXTRACT 1
Nunan, D. 1988. *Syllabus Design* pp. 56–7. Oxford: Oxford University Press.

EXTRACT 2
Abbs, B. *et al.* 1978. *Challenges: Students' Book* pp. 2–14. London: Longman.

EXTRACT 3
Nunan, D. 1982. *What Do You Think?* Adelaide: Language Press.

EXTRACT 4
Hover, D. 1986. *Think Twice* pp. 45–8. Cambridge: Cambridge University Press.

EXTRACT 5
Hamp-Lyons, L., and B. Heasley. 1987. *Study Writing* pp. 8–19. Cambridge: Cambridge University Press.

EXTRACT 6
Nunan, D., and J. Lockwood. 1988. *The Australian English Course: Level 1. Draft Pilot Edition.* Cambridge: Cambridge University Press.

Appendix A

Extract 1

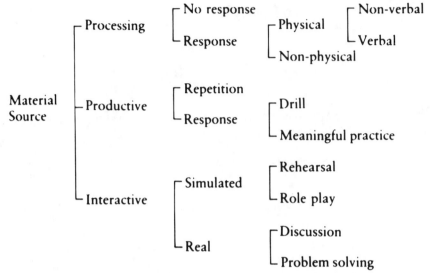

Figure 1: Activity type categorized according to learner responses (*Nunan 1985*)

Material Source

Interview adapted from an authentic source

Interviewer: Have you got a family, Doris?
Doris: Family? Yeah, I've got a family all right. My father's still alive. His name's Jack. He's still with us all right.
Interviewer: What about your husband?
Doris: Bert. That's my husband. That's him in the photo, there.
Interviewer: I see. What about children?
Doris: Three, I've got three children. Two sons and a daughter. The sons are Peter and Jack, and my daughter's called Nancy. Nancy's the youngest — she's only eighteen.

Activities

Level 1: Processing

Response: physical, non-verbal
Pre-teach the words 'father', 'husband', 'sons', 'daughter'. Play the tape. Every time students hear these words they put up their hands.

Response: non-physical, non-verbal
Pre-teach the words 'father', 'husband', 'sons', 'daughter'. Students sight read the words on the grid. Play the tape. Every time students hear the words they place a tick in the appropriate box.

father	
mother	
sons	
daughter	

Response: non-physical, non-verbal
Pre-teach the words 'father', 'husband', 'sons', 'daughter'.
Give the students a written gapped version of the text. Play the tape and get students to fill in the gaps.

Level 2: Productive

Repetition
Get students to listen and repeat.
Cue: Have you got a family?
           Have you got any children?
           Have you got a son?
           Have you got a daughter?

Response: drill
Get students to listen and complete.
Cue: Have you got a family (any children)?
Response: Have you got any children?
Cue: a son
Response: Have you got a son?
Cue: a daughter
Response: Have you got a daughter?
Cue: an uncle
Response: Have you got an uncle?
           etc.

Response: meaningful practice
Put students into pairs and get them to ask and answer questions using cue cards.
A Have you got (a/an/any) _____ ? family/ children/ son
                                      daughter/ uncle/ aunt/
                                      niece/ nephew

≫→

Level 3: Interactive

Simulated: role-play
Give each student a role card which contains a persona and a family tree. Students have to circulate and find members of their family.

Real: discussion
Put students into small groups and ask them to take turns at describing their families using the structures already practised.

Real: problem solving
Students are given a blank family tree. They are split into three groups, and each group hears an incomplete description of the family.
They work together to fill in their part of the family tree and then join with members of other groups to complete the family tree.

Extract 2

Searching and Sharing

BRITISH BROADCASTING CORPORATION

BBC/Challenges Research Notes

STEP 1 READING

<u>CHARLOTTE</u>

Charlotte is 18 years old and works as a receptionist in Oxford Street in London's West End. She is a pretty girl with a lively personality. She gets on well with people and has a lot of friends.

At present, Charlotte has no fixed address. She has been looking for somewhere to live for about three months. So far she has been unsuccessful and has been sleeping on the floor of a friend's flat.

Charlottes's parents live in the country just outside London and although it is possible to live at home with her parents and commute to London every day to work like thousands of other people, Charlotte wants to be independent. She wants to lead a life of her own.

Charlotte's boyfriend, Glen, shares a flat with three other friends. They were lucky. They found a flat very quickly. Charlotte, however, has not been so lucky.

Every day she buys an evening paper and looks through the advertisements. She visits and telephones Flat Agencies about three times a week. She buys a magazine called 'Time Out' every Thursday and looks through the 'Flats to Share' pages very carefully.

She has been to see a number of different places in different parts of London. Each time she has been disappointed for one reason or another.

STEP 2 QUESTIONNAIRE

You are the person who interviews Charlotte at a flat agency. Fill in the form for her using the information in the text.

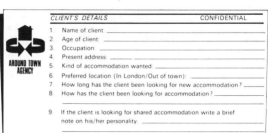

AROUND TOWN
AGENCY

CLIENT'S DETAILS	CONFIDENTIAL
1. Name of client:	
2. Age of client:	
3. Occupation:	
4. Present address:	
5. Kind of accommodation wanted:	
6. Preferred location (In London/Out of town):	
7. How long has the client been looking for new accommodation?	
8. How has the client been looking for accommodation?	
9. If the client is looking for shared accommodation write a brief note on his/her personality.	

STEP 3 WRITING

Tell the story of Charlotte's search. Fill in the gaps using a suitable form of the words in brackets.

When Charlotte left home she .... (go) to stay with friends in London. She first .... (consult) an agent. Then she .... (visit) a flat which a 50-year-old woman .... (want) to share. The following morning she .... (phone) about another room. When she .... (get) there, she .... (find) that the room was very tiny. And she .... (not like) the girl there. She ... . (call at) another flat, but she was too late. They had found someone. Next she .... (ring) a boy who lived in a bed-sitter. But the bed-sitter .... (not suit) her either. She .... (begin) to feel very depressed. Then a friend .... (read) her an advertisement from the newspaper. The people .... (want) someone to share a relaxed, happy flat. Charlotte .... (phone) them. The girls .... (interview) her and another girl. They .... (choose) Charlotte. The next Saturday she .... (move in).

Appendix A

STEP 4 READING

These advertisements come from a copy of 'Time Out' Charlotte read one day.

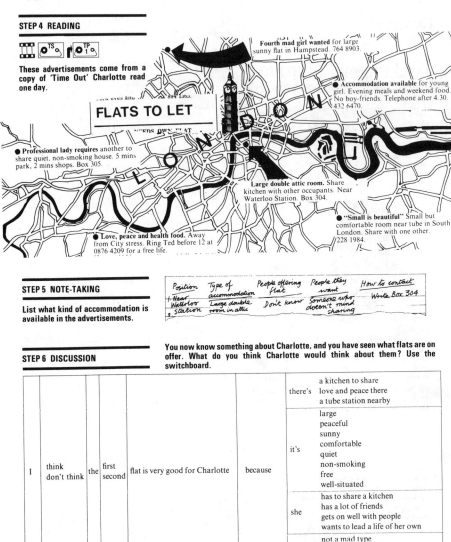

FLATS TO LET

● **Fourth mad girl wanted** for large sunny flat in Hampstead. 764 8903.

● **Accommodation available** for young girl. Evening meals and weekend food. No boy-friends. Telephone after 4.30. 432 6470.

● **Professional lady requires** another to share quiet, non-smoking house. 5 mins park, 2 mins shops. Box 305.

Large double attic room. Share kitchen with other occupants. Near Waterloo Station. Box 304.

● **"Small is beautiful"** Small but comfortable room near tube in South London. Share with one other. 228 1984.

● **Love, peace and health food.** Away from City stress. Ring Ted before 12 at 0876 4209 for a free life.

STEP 5 NOTE-TAKING

List what kind of accommodation is available in the advertisements.

Position	Type of accommodation	People offering flat	People they want	How to contact
1 Near Waterloo Station	Large double room in attic	Don't know	Someone who doesn't mind sharing	Write Box 304
2				

STEP 6 DISCUSSION

You now know something about Charlotte, and you have seen what flats are on offer. What do you think Charlotte would think about them? Use the switchboard.

I	think / don't think	the	first / second	flat is very good for Charlotte	because	there's	a kitchen to share / love and peace there / a tube station nearby
						it's	large / peaceful / sunny / comfortable / quiet / non-smoking / free / well-situated
						she	has to share a kitchen / has a lot of friends / gets on well with people / wants to lead a life of her own
						she's	not a mad type / too young / 18 / lively

152

TASK 1

Now tell your group what you think about the flats.

I	like don't like prefer	the	first second	flat	because	I'm .... it's .... there's .... there isn't ....

TASK 2

You have arrived in an English-speaking country. You are looking for a flat, perhaps alone, perhaps to share with somebody. Write an advertisement for the newspaper asking for accommodation. Your advertisement might look something like these:

Please insert my small-ad for .... week(s) in the .... section of CLASSIFIED. First insert date to be .... If received too late for publication on this day, please insert my ad. in the following edition YES/NO

French	girl,	studying	at
University,	needs	small	flat
for	rent	January.	Sitting
room,	Bedroom,	Bathroom,	kitchen.
Maximum	- £25	a	week.
Phone	42709		

> FOREIGN STUDENT, man, 30 years old, seeks flat to share, preferably with Englishman, Town Centre. Cooking facilities essential. Write Box No. 789.

STEP 1 LISTENING

When Charlotte was looking for a flat she often had to phone. On one occasion the line was very bad. Listen to this conversation between someone who advertised a flat in 'Time Out' and Lawrence, who was looking for a flat.

STEP 2 TRUE OR FALSE?

Make sure that you have understood: do the True/False Exercise, putting crosses in the right boxes.

	TRUE	FALSE
Lawrence wanted to see the flat in the evening.		
Lawrence didn't know where Ealing is.		
The nearest tube station to the flat was North Ealing.		
When you leave the tube station you turn left.		
The flat is in the third street on the left from the tube station.		
The flat is half-way along the street.		
He told Lawrence to come at 7 o'clock.		

Appendix A

STEP 3 LISTENING + NOTE-TAKING

Listen to the phone conversation again. Sometimes Lawrence says that he hasn't heard what the other person is saying. How does he ask him to repeat what he said? Make notes.

When someone repeats something, they don't use the same words. Write down what they said the first time and the second time, like this:

HOW TO SHOW YOU
HAVEN'T HEARD
Sorry, I couldn't hear you

HOW TO REPEAT THINGS
I'd like to, yes — I said I'd
like to, yes.

TASK

Now complete this telephone conversation. Try to use some of the expressions you have noted down.

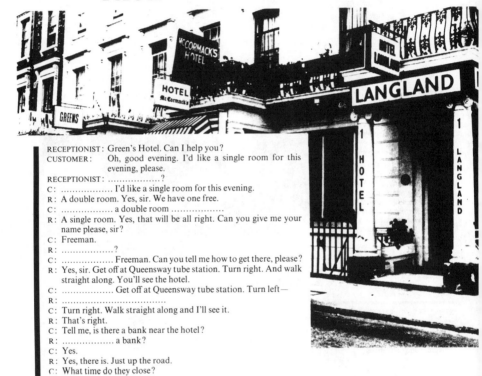

RECEPTIONIST : Green's Hotel. Can I help you?
CUSTOMER : Oh, good evening. I'd like a single room for this evening, please.
RECEPTIONIST : ....?
C : .... I'd like a single room for this evening.
R : A double room. Yes, sir. We have one free.
C : .... a double room ....
R : A single room. Yes, that will be all right. Can you give me your name please, sir?
C : Freeman.
R : ....?
C : .... Freeman. Can you tell me how to get there, please?
R : Yes, sir. Get off at Queensway tube station. Turn right. And walk straight along. You'll see the hotel.
C : .... Get off at Queensway tube station. Turn left—
R : ....
C : Turn right. Walk straight along and I'll see it.
R : That's right.
C : Tell me, is there a bank near the hotel?
R : .... a bank?
C : Yes.
R : Yes, there is. Just up the road.
C : What time do they close?
R : Just up the road, sir.
C : .... do they close?
R : At 3.30, sir.
C : Well, thanks. I'll be along straight away.

154

chain C

STEP 1 LISTENING

Listen to the conversation between a flat agent and someone who is looking for somewhere to live. As you listen, look at the chart. The chart gives information about the accommodation available.

CITY ACCOMMODATION SERVICE				ACCOMMODATION AVAILABLE
Address	**SHARED FLATS**		**BED-SITTERS**	
	16 April Place	14 North Road	6 Elm Street	2 Cambridge Square
Own room		✓	✓	
Shared room	✓			✓
Good public transport	✗	✓	✓	✗
Garden	✗	✓	✗	✓
Cooking facilities	✓	✓	✗	✓
Furnished	✓		✓	✓
Unfurnished		✓		
Number of people in house/flat	4	3	6	8
Price	£16	£20	£12	£10
Notes	No telephone Non-smokers only	Gets cold in winter	No animals allowed	Please provide own bed linen

STEP 2 PAIRWORK: INTERVIEWS

Work in pairs, as a flat agent and a client. First read the conversation about the accommodation available at 16 April Place. Then look at the information about shared flats and bed-sitters available at the City Accommodation Service and act similar dialogues for 14 North Road, 6 Elm Street and 2 Cambridge Square.

CLIENT: I'm looking for somewhere to live.
AGENT: Now do you want a shared flat or a bed-sitter?
CLIENT: I'd like to *share a flat*.
AGENT: Right, well, what about this one—it's at *16 April Place*.
CLIENT: Would I be able to have my own room?
AGENT: *No, I'm afraid you'd have to share a room.*
CLIENT: And what about cooking facilities? Are they available?
AGENT: *Yes, they are.*
CLIENT: Is it furnished?
AGENT: *Yes, it is.*
CLIENT: Oh, and has it got a garden? *I like gardening.*
AGENT: *No, I'm afraid it hasn't.*
CLIENT: Oh! And what about public transport? Are the transport services good in the area?
AGENT: *No, not very, I'm afraid.*
CLIENT: Perhaps you could tell me how many other people would be in the same place.
AGENT: Let me have a look. Oh, yes, there would be *3 other people*.
CLIENT: And the price . . . how much is the rent per week?
AGENT: *£16 per week*. Oh, and there's one more thing I should tell you—*there isn't a telephone. And they want a non-smoker*.
CLIENT: Well, thank you very much for your information. I'll think about it and telephone you this afternoon to tell you if I want to have a look at the place.
AGENT: Fine! I'll expect to hear from you.

155

STEP 3 LISTENING

Listen to the conversation again; this time, as you listen, look at the form provided by the City Accommodation Service for people who are looking for somewhere to live.

CITY ACCOMMODATION SERVICE

FORM FOR CLIENTS

The information you give us on this form will help us find the right accommodation for you.

NAME _____
ADDRESS _____ _____ _____ TELEPHONE _____

Please write Yes or No in the boxes

1a Separate flat	☐
1b Shared flat (with people of own age and interests)	☐
Own Room	☐
Shared Room	☐
1c Bed-sitter	☐
Own Room	☐
Shared Room	☐
2 Cooking facilities	
Shared kitchen	
Use of small gas or electric cooker	☐
3 Furnished	
Unfurnished	☐
4 Use of garden	☐
5 Good public transport (near bus, train or underground routes)	☐
6 Location	
Town or city centre	☐
Suburbs	☐
Country	☐
7 Other requirements: Please indicate below any other requirements you may have.	

_____
_____
_____

Signed: Date:

STEP 4 PAIRWORK: INTERVIEWS

Now complete the client's form for your partner. Ask and answer about each part of the form like this:

AGENT	CLIENT
What sort of accommodation would you prefer?	I'd prefer a ....
Would you like your own room or would you like to share a room?	I'd like ....
What sort of cooking facilities would you like?	I'd like ....
Do you want furnished or un-furnished accommodation?	I want ....
Would you like to use a garden?	Yes, I .... No, I don't need ....
Do you need public transport?	....
What sort of location are you interested in?	I'd like to live in ....
Have you any other requirements?	Yes, I must have .... Yes, I need to have .... No, I haven't got any other requirements.

TASK 1

With your own requirements and the list of accommodation available you can act the situation when YOU visit the flat agency. The person who is the flat agent will try to suggest suitable accommodation from the available information.

CLIENT: I'm looking for somewhere to live.
AGENT: I see. Which would you prefer: a shared flat or a bed-sitter?
CLIENT: I'd prefer a ....
AGENT: Now let's have a look. Ah, here's one, it's at ....
         (choose one of the places and continue)

TASK 2

You are going to live in England. Write to an estate agent to ask for some suitable accommodation for yourself and your family. Use the information that you gave to the City Accommodation Agency to help you compose your letter. Start your letter like letter 1.

Change letters with your partner and write a reply, making an offer of suitable accommodation. Start your letter like letter 2.

1

Dear Sir,
I shall be coming to live in England from............ and I would be extremely grateful if your agency could find me somewhere suitable to live. I would like to have ....

2

CITY ACCOMMODATION SERVICE

Dear Mr/Mrs/Miss/Ms ......

    Thank you for your letter of.............. about accommodation. I have considered your requirements carefully and find that I have the following suitable accommodation available. The address is..............
........and it is....................................

chain d

STEP 1 LISTENING

Listen to John talking about the flat he used to live in. You will find out lots of things about him. Check them off on the chart.

CHARACTERISTICS	TRUE	FALSE
He likes peace and quiet		
He's tidy		
He always goes around with a crowd of people		
He is kind and sympathetic		
He never goes to bed early		
He likes classical music		
He's fussy about his food		
He likes talking about himself		

STEP 2 MATCHING

Now try to put John's various characteristics under the following headings:

Likes	Dislikes	Habits

STEP 3 NOTE-MAKING

Most people share living accommodation at some time in their life; it's important to know if you can get on with others. First work alone. Decide about your own characteristics. Use the same headings as in Step 2 and make notes about yourself.

STEP 4 PAIRWORK: DISCUSSION

Exchange your notes from Step 3 with a partner and decide whether he or she would be able to share somewhere to live with John. See what your partner thinks about your opinion.

157

TASK 1

Find a person to share a flat. This is what you do:

1. Make groups of four.
2. Make pairs within your group.
3. Take it in turns to interview the other pair. Decide which person you would rather live with.

These are the things you should try to ask questions about:

People's likes, dislikes, preferences, personality and people's personal characteristics. These language lists will help you:

What do you enjoy doing?	I enjoy ....
What do you like?	I like ....
What don't you like?	I don't like ....
Do you mind ....?	I don't mind .... too much.
It's all right if .... isn't it?	Of course it's all right if ....
Is there anything you can't stand?	I can't stand .... but I can put up with ....
Would you say that you are .....?	Well, I think I'm ....

TASK 2

You have been invited as a guest by an English family. Write a friendly letter introducing and describing yourself.

PROJECT

QUESTIONNAIRE

Name _____

Address _____

Occupation _____

Married/Single _____

Number of children _____

Type of Accommodation	House/Flat/Room/Shared Room
Number of rooms	
Is the accommodation shared?	Yes/No
If yes:	
Would you prefer to live alone?	Yes/No
Do you get on with the other people?	Yes/No
Is there a separate bathroom?	Yes/No
Do you have a separate room of your own for sleep, study or entertaining friends?	Yes/No
Would you consider your accommodation	Ideal/Good/ Reasonable/Bad?
Do you like the area you live in?	Yes/No
Is your accommodation well situated for	
Transport?	Yes/No
Shops, etc.?	Yes/No
Recreation facilities?	Yes/No
Access to country?	Yes/No
If you could, would you prefer to live somewhere else?	Yes/No
If yes:	
Where would you prefer to live?	
Why would you like to move?	

The Way We Live Now
– a survey of people's living conditions

Make a survey of the living conditions of the people in your class or group, or people you live near.

Use English to interview people in your group, but use your own language if you are interviewing other people in your own country.

Interview people by following the questions on the questionnaire. You can add other questions if you think they are relevant.

Collect the information from your interviews on the TOTALS AND PERCENTAGES sheet on the next page.

Put your individual findings together and prepare a REPORT, like the one on the next page. The underlined words may be useful for your reports.

PROJECT

TOTALS AND PERCENTAGES

THE WAY WE LIVE NOW. RESULTS OF SURVEY
OF PEOPLE'S LIVING CONDITIONS

	No.	%
People interviewed		
Married people with one or more children		
Single people		
People living in houses		
People living in flats		
People living in bed-sitters		
People living in shared accommodation		
People with separate bathroom		
People with a room of their own		
People who consider their accommodation ideal or good		
People who consider their accommodation bad		
People who like the area they live in		
People well situated for transport		
People well situated for recreational facilities		
People well situated for access to the country		
People who would prefer to live somewhere else		

REPORT ON THE SURVEY

Report: The Way We Live
Area of survey: Leeds
Type of Group interviewed: Students
Date of interview: 20th October

In our survey we interviewed 24 people. They were all
students and were single.

16 people we interviewed live in a house and seven people
live in a flat. One student lives in a room alone. His
parents have moved to another town. As he wanted to stay,
his parents gave him money to rent a room here. Except
for this one person everybody lives with their family.
There is nothing significant about the number of people
who have a separate kitchen, but one thing interested us
a lot - the number of people who didn't have a room of
their own. The percentage of people with a room of their
own was very low - 22%. One result was expected: this
was the percentage of people who found their accommodation
not very good - 50%. Many said that they would prefer to
live in or nearer the country because they felt that
their neighbourhood suffered from air and noise pollution.
A large number of people said that they must have peace
and quiet. They said they would move if it were financially
possible.

Living and Leaving

chain e

STEP 1 ANALYSIS

What is a home? Some people really
like equipment or gadgets: they say
'a home is what you have in it'. Here
is a list of household equipment or
gadgets which are easily available,
and which some people think important. Do you think they are?

APPLIANCE	USELESS	USEFUL	ESSENTIAL
Electric frying pan			
Electric toaster			
Electric kettle			
Dishwasher			
Washing machine			
Vacuum cleaner			
Air conditioning			
Food mixer			
Ice-cream maker			
Deep-freeze			
Refrigerator			
Electric toothbrush			
Hi-fi system			
Hairdryer			
Electric knife sharpener			
Electric juice extractor			
Colour TV			

Appendix A

STEP 2 REPORTING

Now tell your group what you think. Use the switchboard:

I think	most nearly all a lot a few hardly any almost none	of these things	are	useless useful essential

STEP 3 GROUPWORK: DISCUSSION

Discuss with the members of your group the articles you think are useless, useful or essential. Be prepared to give reasons for your opinion. The language chart below should help you.

I think the .... In my opinion the	is	useless useful essential	because ....

I'd want a .... I'd like a .... I wouldn't want a	in my home	because ....

STEP 4 PAIRWORK: DISCUSSION

It's not often that we find exactly the ideal place to live and very often we can't afford exactly what we want to furnish the place we live in. We often have to accept something that's not perfect, and make the best of it.
Look at the plan of a flat, a store of furniture to go with it and a list of extra things you could buy.
With a partner, decide how you would arrange the flat and what you would buy. You have £100 to spend. These expressions might be useful in your discussion.

Let's ....
What about putting ....
What do you think of ....
I think we should ....
Shall we ....
Perhaps the best thing would be to
....
Can't you/we ....
No, you can't possibly put ....
Why don't you/we ....
Everybody puts ....
Well, couldn't we ....
If I were you I'd ....

THINGS TO BUY		Price
Article	Price New	Second Hand
Fridge	£75	£10
Standard Lamp	£14	£6.50
Bookshelf	£17	£4.75
Sofa	£129.95	£25
Desk Lamp	£10.95	£3
Posters	£1.20	–
Ready-made curtains	£33	£6
Stereo	£215.45	£45
TV	£99.75	£16.80
Bed	£69.95	£13

STEP 5 MATCHING

Now look at these expressions. Decide which expressions fit which intentions.

I put the .... near the ....

I thought I needed a ....
I wanted a ....
I decided to buy a ....

Great!
That's a good idea!

You can't put it there!
Not there!

You didn't need a ....
......., did you?

A .... wasn't necessary, was it?

Why?
Why not?

Well, I like it
I don't agree with you
That's not what I think

Because ....

SAY IT WAS A BAD IDEA

SAY YOU THINK IT'S GOOD

GIVE REASONS

SAY YOU AGREE

SAY YOU DISAGREE

SAY WHERE YOU PUT SOMETHING

SAY WHAT YOU DECIDED TO BUY

ASK WHY

ASK WHY NOT

SAY SOMETHING WASN'T NECESSARY

STEP 6 DISCUSSION

When you have decided how you want your flat, discuss the arrangement with a partner or in groups. Use the chart.

SAY WHERE YOU PUT SOMETHING	SAY YOU THINK IT'S GOOD				AGREE
	SAY YOU THINK IT'S NOT GOOD	ASK WHY NOT	GIVE REASONS		
SAY WHAT YOU DECIDED TO BUY	SAY YOU THINK IT'S GOOD				DISAGREE
	SAY SOMETHING WASN'T NECESSARY	ASK WHY			

TASK

Imagine you have just been shopping. Use the chart and discuss with your partner what you have bought. Simulate different kinds of situations where someone tells other people what he/she has bought.

STEP 1 READING

Home means many different things to different people.

The Kitchen

... our waking life, and our growing years, were for the most part spent in the kitchen, and until we married, or ran away, it was the common room we shared. Here we lived and fed in a family fug, not minding the little space, trod on each other like birds in a hole, elbowed our ways without spite, all talking at once or all silent at once, or crying against each other, but never I think feeling overcrowded, being as separate as notes in a scale. . . .
... Walking downstairs there was a smell of floorboards, of rags, sour lemons, old spices. The smoky kitchen was in its morning muddle, from which breakfast would presently emerge. Mother stirred the porridge in a soot-black pot. Tony was carving bread with a ruler, the girls in their mackintoshes were laying the table, and the cats were eating the butter. I cleaned some boots and pumped up some fresh water; Jack went for a jug of skimmed milk.

From: Laurie Lee 'Cider with Rosie'

Appendix A

STEP 2 WRITING

Laurie and his .... spent most of the .... in the kitchen. They lived there and .... there. There wasn't much ... . but they never felt overcrowded. When you walked downstairs you could smell the wooden .... , and other smells. The kitchen was full of .... , and in the morning was always in a .... Breakfast would soon be .... Mother was stirring the porridge in a pot blackened by the .... Tony was carving the bread with a ruler instead of a .... The girls were wearing .... as they .... Laurie went to the .... for some fresh water and Jack collected some skimmed milk in a ....

STEP 3 LISTENING + PAIRWORK

What does home mean to you?
First listen to different people describing what home means to them. Then work in pairs. Ask your partner the following questions and fill in his/her answers.

STEP 4 ANALYSIS

Look at your partner's answers to the questions and summarise what you think his/her answers suggest about his/her ideas about 'home'.

STEP 5 NOTE-MAKING

Look at all the points you have answered 'yes' to and write them down in what you think is their order of importance.

STEP 6 GROUPWORK: REPORT

Analyse the results of the investigation in a large group. Do this by asking:

Do you think a home is somewhere	Yes	No	Don't know
you are secure and warm?			
you can be alone?			
you can keep all your possessions?			
you can bring up a family?			
you can entertain your friends and relatives?			
you can make a noise?			
you can do what you want?			
you can be in love?			
you can die in peace?			
you can look after your parents?			

Do you think a home is something			
you can make beautiful?			
you can keep clean?			
you can show off to your friends?			
that will give you financial security?			
that everybody needs?			

How many people think that a home *is* somewhere you are secure and warm.
How many people think that a home *isn't* somewhere you are secure and warm.
How many people don't know about this point?

Write a brief report on the results of your investigation. Use phrases like this:

Most people think that a home is . . .
A few people think that . . .
Hardly anyone thinks that . . .
No one thinks that . . .

162

STEP 7 READING

Not everybody leaves home because they want to as Charlotte did. Read these Social Worker's Case Notes.

Jean Willis *CASE NOTES* STRICTLY CONFIDENTIAL

Jean left school when she was sixteen. She had a job as a waitress for one year, then lost it. Her family relationships are not happy. There are seven brothers and sisters. Her mother is divorced from her father. She has remarried. Jean's stepfather tried to assault her several times when drunk. The mother is unhappy in her second marriage, and also drinks. It is understandable that Jean didn't want to stay at home.

She ran away to London three months ago. When she left home she had £6.50. This went in one day. She wandered round town, and ended up at Piccadilly Circus. There she met other young people who had no home in a slot-machine arcade. She lived with them for a week in a ruined house in Wimbledon.

After leaving there she started to sleep in parks, back streets, or cars with open doors.

She was referred to me by Dr. Noakes. She is two months pregnant. She states that she does not wish to return home.

Signed: *M. L. Brooks*

TASK

You almost certainly don't have serious problems like Jean had. But there are probably things in your life which do annoy you or make you angry. Note down 3 or 4 of these things. Then work in small groups and discuss them. The different members of the group may have interesting or helpful suggestions.

chang

STEP 1 LISTENING + NOTE-TAKING

Listen to the different people talking on the tape. They have all left their own countries to live somewhere else.
Make notes about the things they talk about; about who they are and what they miss. These headings will help you.

STEP 2 NOTE-MAKING

STEP 3 PAIRWORK: REPORTING

Use the notes that you made in Step 2 and tell your partner what you would miss.
These sentences and phrases may help you:

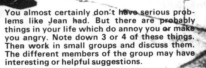

PEOPLE WEATHER
SIGHTS AND ENVIRONMENT
POSSESSIONS
FAMILY AND FRIENDS FOOD
EVERYDAY ROUTINES
NATIONAL OR RELIGIOUS FESTIVALS

Imagine that you have decided to leave your home and country. Think of all the things you would miss. Make notes with the same headings as in Step 1.

If I left my country I'd miss . . .
There are some things which you can only get in my country—for example . . .
There are some special days I would miss, particularly . . .
Most of all I would miss . . . because . . .

Appendix A

Extract 3

This unit of work is based on an information gap task. After some preliminary vocabulary work, the class is divided into three. Each group hears a different tape, takes notes, and answers some comprehension questions. They then regroup. The new groups consist of a representative from each of the three original groups. They then share their information and use it to complete the task of drawing the floor plan of the house they have heard described.

Plan the House

The problem

The three tapes in this unit describe various parts of a house. The problem for the students is to integrate the information presented in the texts and produce a floor plan of the house.

Vocabulary and idioms

the goods	renovating
ornate	either way
waffle	fibro
to be sold on	to pop across
come good	

Instructions

Give a general introduction to the unit and explain the problem to be solved. Explain vocabulary and idiomatic expressions.

Whole class:
Follow the format provided in the introduction.

Small groups:
1. Divide the class into three groups.
2. Give each group a cassette player and one of the conversations.
3. Ask students to listen to the tape and answer the questions.
4. Rearrange the class into new groups containing a student from each of the original groups and ask them to fill in the information table.
5. Using the data from the information table, students are to draw a plan of the house.
6. Get students to return to their original groups and compare plans.
7. Let the whole class listen to all three texts.
8. Show students the solution provided in the teacher's book and discuss variations.

INFORMATION TABLE

	Text 1	*Text 2*	*Text 3*
Bedrooms			
Lounge/Dining room			
Kitchen			
Bathroom/Toilet			
Hall			
Sunroom			
Study			
Storeroom			
Laundry			
Verandah			
Garden			

Plan the House

The problem

In this activity, you will hear someone describing a house. Your task is to use the information you hear to draw a floor plan of the house which is described.

Vocabulary and idioms

the goods	to be sold on	either way
ornate	come good	fibro
waffle	renovating	to pop across

Instructions

1. Listen to the tape and answer the questions relating to the conversation you heard. You may replay the tape as often as you need in order to find answers to the questions.
2. In recombined groups, discuss each of the tapes and then fill in the information table.

165

3. Using the data from the information table, draw a plan of the house.
4. Return to your original groups and compare plans.
5. Study the solution provided to the teacher and discuss any variations.

Text 1

A message from Michael Mullins to his wife.

Well, good news at last. After looking at about 200 houses, I've managed to come up with the goods. I reckon I've found just the place for us. It's in Blackwood, which is an outer suburb about 25 minutes drive from the city. I think you'll love it. It's got a lovely big garden and lots of trees.

The house itself is about 60 years old, so it's quite stylish with high ornate ceilings, open fireplaces and polished wooden floors. It's really peaceful, loads of charm, too, and I'm sure you'll find it delightful.

Anyway, enough of the waffle. The house is basically a three bedroom bungalow, a country style house with wide verandahs and all that. It could easily be converted into four bedrooms if we wanted. In fact it was four bedrooms once, the fourth bedroom running off the lounge room. The last owner removed part of the dividing wall between the lounge and bedroom to make a very spacious lounge/dining room. We could always replace the wall if we wanted an extra bedroom or a study.

What sold me on the house was the kitchen. It leads off the lounge/dining room and is huge. There's a large workbench in the middle of the room, and there's also room for a kitchen table. We can eat in there when we don't feel like having a formal meal in the dining room. Oh yes, and there's a walk-in pantry in one corner of the kitchen.

Off the kitchen, you know, at the back of the house, are two rooms. These are side-by-side and each has its own door leading into the kitchen. The room on the left would make a useful study or family room. The one on the right, which has a wine cellar by the way, would be a very good store room or junk room.

I'd better finish now. I'm off to the bank to see whether they'll come good with a loan. Oh, I forgot to tell you the price. They're asking a very reasonable 65 thousand.

Text 1 questions

1. Where is the house?
2. How old is the house?
3. How many bedrooms has it got?
4. What did the previous owner do to the lounge room?
5. Which room did Mr Mullins like best?
6. Why?
7. What is there in one corner of the kitchen?
8. What runs off the kitchen?
9. How much is the house?

Text 2

A telephone conversation between Michael Mullins and his wife.

M: Hello, Ruth?
R: Hi!
M: Great news about the house wasn't it?
R: Yes, fantastic. Now tell me all about it.
M: Well, as I said, it's basically a three bedroom house. Very individual in style. There's no front door at all, and the hall runs across the house instead of down it. You come into the hall from a side door. As you walk down the hall, there're two bedrooms on the left. On the right is a door leading into this huge lounge/dining room.
R: What about the third bedroom?
M: Well, if you keep going down the hall, it's on the right, past the lounge room. There's a lovely open fireplace in the wall that separates the lounge room from the third bedroom.
R: What about outside?
M: Well, there's a big wide verandah running across the front of the house. The two main bedrooms look out onto this. It also continues down the left-hand side of the house. Part of it, on the western side, is enclosed, making a kind of sunroom.
R: Which, I suppose, could be used as an extra bedroom if necessary.
M: Yes, except that the sunroom acts as a passage to the bathroom and toilet.
R: I see.
M: One of the nicest things about the place is the enormous garden. A driveway runs down the left-hand side of the house to the garden. On the right of the house is an orchard with apple, plum and orange trees. At the rear is a large grassed area surrounded by a border of trees and shrubs. In the middle of the lawn is an old clothes line.
R: That'll have to go!
M: Well, they are useful.
R: I don't care, they're ugly.
M: OK, the clothes line goes.
R: Well, then, when can I see it?
M: As soon as you arrive tomorrow.
R: Great. I'll see you then.

Text 2 questions

1. What is Mr Mullins's good news?
2. How many bedrooms has the house got?
3. What is unusual about the hall?
4. Which rooms lead off the hall to the left?
5. Which rooms lead off to the right?
6. What runs across the front of the house?
7. How would you describe the garden?
8. What is in the middle of the lawn?

Text 3

A message from Drew Well, Architect to Jack Hammer, Builder.

Jack, I've just looked at a house in Blackwood for a Mr Michael Mullins who wants some renovating done. It's a nice old rambling place – about 60 years old at a guess, so there's a bit of work to be done as you might imagine. Still, it's solid enough. There're two rooms off the kitchen at the back of the house. One of these is currently a study. The owner wants these two rooms knocked down and a family room built. Apart from demolishing the two rooms, the cellar'll have to be filled in and one of the doors'll have to be blocked up. (This can either be the doorway from the kitchen to the study or the doorway from the kitchen to the store room – doesn't matter much either way.)

The other major job concerns rebuilding the sunroom, bathroom/toilet and laundry. The sunroom's on the left of the house. It used to be part of the verandah, but was closed in years ago – it's only fibro, so knocking it down shouldn't be a problem. The bathroom and toilet lead off the sunroom and run across the back of the house. Between the bathroom/toilet on the left and the kitchen on the right is the laundry. At present, to get to the bathroom or toilet, you either have to go down the main hall into the sunroom and then into the bathroom, or you have to go through the kitchen and then the laundry. Mr Mullins would like the bathroom and toilet nearer the bedrooms.

Anyway, I'd be obliged if you could pop across sometime, have a look at the house and tell me what you think.

Text 3 questions

1. What has Mr Well just done?
2. How old is the house?
3. What runs off the kitchen?
4. What are these used for?
5. What does the owner want done with them?
6. What will have to be done with the cellar?
7. What is the second major job?
8. Where are the bathroom/toilet located?
9. Where would the owner like the toilet to be relocated?

INFORMATION TABLE — KEY

	Text 1	*Text 2*	*Text 3*
Bedrooms	3 bedrooms	3 bedrooms 2 on left of hall 1 on right past lounge	
Lounge/dining room	Very spacious. Constructed from former lounge and 4th bedroom.	Huge. On right from hall. Open fire place in wall between lounge and 3rd bedroom.	
Kitchen	Leads off lounge/dining room. Huge, large workbench in middle. Room for kitchen table. Walk-in pantry.		
Bathroom/Toilet		Off sunroom.	Off sunroom.
Hall		Runs across the house.	
Sunroom		Made up from verandah. Acts as passage to bathroom/ toilet.	On left of house. Was part of verandah.
Study	Off kitchen on left. Next to storeroom.		Off back of kitchen.
Storeroom	Off kitchen on right. Next to study.		Off back of kitchen. Has cellar.
Laundry			Between bathroom/ toilet and kitchen.

Appendix A

	Text 1	*Text 2*	*Text 3*
Verandah	Wide.	Runs across front of house and down left-hand side.	
Garden	Big – lots of trees.	Enormous. Orchard.	

Activity sheet

Below is an outline of the house. Use the information in the information table to produce a plan of the house.

Plan the House

Extension activity

Give students advertisements from the real estate pages of the newspaper and get them to draw floor plans of the houses described.

Provide students with a number of floor plans and get them to write newspaper advertisements for these houses.

The solution

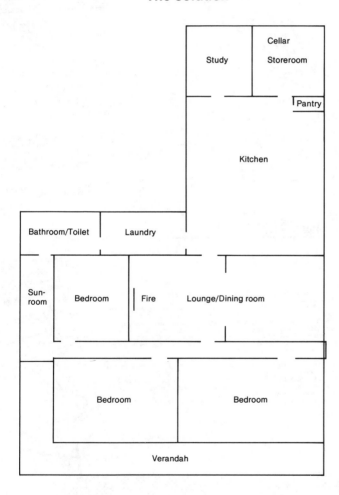

Extract 4

THE HOUSING COMMITTEE ⧹ 18A

You and your partner work for the City Council in Cambourne, Australia. You are on the Housing Committee. The Housing Committee helps people to find flats and houses.

Anne Littleton and Harry Marden are looking for flats. The information about them is in the letters and the notes. Answer your partner's questions so he can fill in the forms for them.

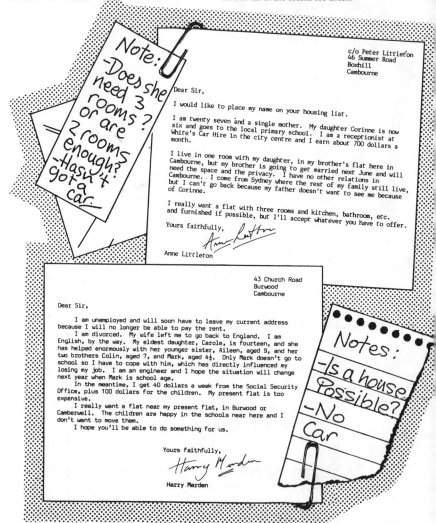

Note:
- Does she need 3 rooms? or are 2 rooms enough?
- Hasn't got a car.

c/o Peter Littleton
46 Summer Road
Boxhill
Cambourne

Dear Sir,

I would like to place my name on your housing list.

I am twenty seven and a single mother. My daughter Corinne is now six and goes to the local primary school. I am a receptionist at White's Car Hire in the city centre and I earn about 700 dollars a month.

I live in one room with my daughter, in my brother's flat here in Cambourne, but my brother is going to get married next June and will need the space and the privacy. I have no other relations in Cambourne. I come from Sydney where the rest of my family still live, but I can't go back because my father doesn't want to see me because of Corinne.

I really want a flat with three rooms and kitchen, bathroom, etc. and furnished if possible, but I'll accept whatever you have to offer.

Yours faithfully,

Anne Littleton

43 Church Road
Burwood
Cambourne

Dear Sir,

I am unemployed and will soon have to leave my current address because I will no longer be able to pay the rent.

I am divorced. My wife left me to go back to England. I am English, by the way. My eldest daughter, Carole, is fourteen, and she has helped enormously with her younger sister, Aileen, aged 9, and her two brothers Colin, aged 7, and Mark, aged 4½. Only Mark doesn't go to school so I have to cope with him, which has directly influenced my losing my job. I am an engineer and I hope the situation will change next year when Mark is school age.

In the meantime, I get 40 dollars a week from the Social Security Office, plus 100 dollars for the children. My present flat is too expensive.

I really want a flat near my present flat, in Burwood or Camberwell. The children are happy in the schools near here and I don't want to move them.

I hope you'll be able to do something for us.

Yours faithfully,

Harry Marden

Notes:
- Is a house Possible?
- No Car

Now look at the houses and flats on page 48. Decide with your partner: Which flat (or house) can you give to Anne Littleton? Harry Marden? What do they *need*?

18A+B / THE HOUSING COMMITTEE

Yuon Hou is looking for a flat. Fill in the form for him.

c/o Phnom Penh Stores
43 Cork Place
Cambourne

Dear Sir

Our home has been destroyed by fire and I do not know where I can turn. My wife, her aunt and our two small children now sleep on the floor of a friend's shop while I sleep in my taxi.

We can pay a fair rent. As you see, I am a taxi driver and I earn 600 dollars a month on average. My wife works three days a week in my friend's shop and earns about 200 dollars a month for this. Ngoc, my eldest son, is seven years old and goes to school. Minh, my other son, is only three and a half years old, so he doesn't go to school yet. My wife's aunt doesn't work because she is too old.

We would like an unfurnished flat. We come from Cambodia, so we like Cambodian furniture, and friends will help us to find that.

Thank you for your interest.

Yours faithfully

Yuon Hou

Yuon Hou

Notes:
- aunt has problems with her back.
Needs ground or 1st floor flat?

HSB 165

CAMBOURNE CITY COUNCIL
HOUSING COMMITTEE

HOUSING REQUEST FORM

first name(s)		age
marital status		
surname	address	
mr/mrs/miss/ms		
nationality		
	place of work	
	other salaries/income	
profession		occupation
salary	age	
dependants		

accommodation wanted

Now look at the houses and flats on page 48. Which flat (or house) can you give to him?

THE HOUSING COMMITTEE 18B

You and your partner work for the City Council in Cambourne, Australia. You are on the Housing Committee. The Housing Committee helps people to find flats or houses.

Anne Littleton and Harry Marden are looking for flats. Your partner has got letters from them with notes. Ask him about them and fill in the forms.

RECEIVED

CAMBOURNE CITY COUNCIL
HOUSING COMMITTEE

HSB 165

HOUSING REQUEST FORM

surname	first name(s)	
mr/mrs/miss/ms	marital status	age
nationality	address	

profession	place of work	
salary	other salaries/income	
dependants	age	occupation

accommodation wanted

CAMBOURNE CITY COUNCIL
HOUSING COMMITTEE

HSB 165

HOUSING REQUEST FORM

surname	first name(s)	
mr/mrs/miss/ms	marital status	age
nationality	address	

profession	place of work	
salary	other salaries/income	
dependants	age	occupation

accommodation wanted

Now look at the houses and flats on page 48 with your partner. Decide together: Which flat (or house) can you give to Anne Littleton? Harry Marden? What do they *need*?

18A + B / THE HOUSING COMMITTEE

Which flat (or house) can you give to Yuon Hou? Anne Littleton? Harry Marden? What exactly do they *need?* Decide with your partner.

**Flat 127
21–23 Avalon Court**
Burwood (suburb)

3 bedrooms, kitchen, living room, toilet, bathroom

6th floor (lift)

Furnished

Car park in front of flats

Shops/schools 1 mile away

Bus to city centre

Rent: 100 dollars/ month

48 Miller's Way
(city centre)

2 bedrooms, kitchen, living room, toilet, bathroom

Ground floor

Unfurnished

Car park near flat

Shops opposite flat/ schools 2 miles away

Rent: 120 dollars/ month

2 Edward Street
Glenroy (suburb)

3 bedrooms, kitchen, living room, toilet, bathroom

4th floor (no lift)

Furnished

No car park

Shops/schools ½ mile away

No bus to centre

Rent: 150 dollars/ month

76 Broad Way
Templestow (suburb)

1 bedroom, kitchen, living room, toilet, bathroom

3rd floor (no lift)

Furnished

Car park next to flats

Near shops / schools 1 mile away

Bus to centre

Rent: 100 dollars/ month

33 Ship Street
Camberwell (suburb)

2 bedrooms, kitchen, living room, toilet, bathroom, garden

Unfurnished

Near small shops / supermarket 2 miles away (bus) / schools 2 miles away (bus)

Bus to city centre

Rent: 160 dollars/ month

Extract 5

PART I

Unit 1 Spatial relationships

Introduction

Very often we have to describe in writing the location of a place, how a place is
laid out or how a set of objects are connected (as in equipment for an
experiment). In this unit we will look at some of the ways of describing spatial
relationships. Spatial descriptions are often accompanied by a visual aid, such as
a plan, map, or diagram.

Task 1

Read the following text by yourself and then look at the map which
accompanies it. With a partner, discuss the text and the map and decide whether
the map helps you to understand the text.

Acidic pollution

The discharge of waste from the
production of titanium dioxide
along the Humber estuary in
Britain causes serious acidification
of local waters, wipes out aquatic
organisms and pollutes the beaches
of Cleethorpes with acid and iron.
The two main titanium dioxide
plants in Britain are BTP Tioxide
of Grimsby and LaPorte Industries
of Stallingborough – both of them
on the Humber estuary. Between
them they discharge more than
60,000 m³ of acidic waste daily. As
a result, a long strip of land along
the south bank of the estuary from
Immingham to Cleethorpes has a
brownish-red colour from the
discharge.

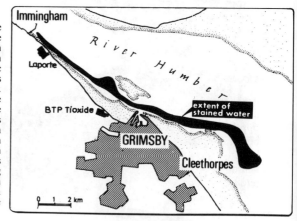

(*New Scientist*)

Not all texts describing spatial relations are accompanied by a map. For
example, the writer of the following text, 'The Abraham Moss Centre', did not
include a map. The text describes the location of a school and is part of the
introduction to an educational research project.

Task 2

Read the passage and then:
a) make a note of the expressions which tell the reader where a place is;
b) using the information in the text, draw a simple map of the area;
c) say what you think the writer's aim was in producing this description;
d) say whether you can draw an accurate map on the basis of the information provided in the passage.

The Abraham Moss Centre

The Abraham Moss Centre is a low, white complex of buildings on the borders of Cheetham and Crumpsall, just to the north of the centre of Manchester. Although the site itself was industrial wasteland, it is in the heart of a residential district. Along one side of it runs a railway, but in every other direction it is surrounded by semi-detached and terraced housing of the inter-war years. Both Cheetham and Crumpsall were fairly prosperous Victorian developments, but Cheetham in particular has undergone extensive redevelopment

---

(A.D. Edwards and V.J. Furlong *The Language of Teaching*)

Some of the expressions in the above text tell you *what* various places are, or were:
'The Abraham Moss Centre is *a low, white complex of buildings*'.
Other expressions tell you *where* various places are, or were:
'The Abraham Moss Centre . . . buildings *on the borders of Cheetham and Crumpsall*'.

Task 3

a) Add as many expressions of spatial relationships as you can to this illustration. Some you could use are:

opposite
between
beside
behind
(etc.)

b) Write four sentences to describe some spatial relationships between objects in the illustration, for example:
The fountain is *in front of* the house.

177

About writing

There are basically two ways of organizing a description of a place. One way is to describe it as if it was being seen from the air (a bird's eye view). The other is to describe it from the point of view of a journey through it (a pedestrian's view). The description may need to be very detailed as, for example, when a novelist is describing a scene; or it can be rather general, as when a student is describing a geographical area as background to an agricultural experiment; or it can be very technical, as when an entomologist is describing the marking on a rare butterfly.

Task 4

Read this text, which describes a geographical area of East Africa, and then, working with another student:
a) decide whether it is written from a bird's eye view or from a pedestrian's view;
b) draw an outline map of the area to accompany the text;
c) decide what changes you would need to make in the text if you rewrote it from the other point of view.

As the Rift Valley sweeps northwards out of Kenya and into Ethiopia, it forms the spectacular Lake Turkana basin. The long, shallow waters of the lake, which stretches 155 miles north to south and up to 35 miles east to west, sparkle green in the tropical sun: someone called it the Jade Sea, a very apt name. At the south a barrier of small volcanic hills prevents the lake spreading further down into the arid lands of northern Kenya. From the west side rises the Rift Valley wall, a range of mountains with some peaks of more than 5000 feet. This is the land of the Turkana people, a tall, elegant pastoralist tribe. Beyond are the mountains and forests of Uganda. Pouring its silt-laden waters into the north end of the lake is the River Omo, a huge river that drains the Ethiopian Highlands to the north, and meanders tortuously as it nears its end at the border with Kenya where it reaches the Jade Sea. Where the river reaches the lake the sudden barrier to its progress forces it to dump its burden of silt, so creating an enormous delta.

(Adapted from R. Leakey and R. Lewin *People of the Lake*)

Task 5

The following text describes the same area as in Task 4, but in a different period of time and from a different point of view. Read the text and draw an outline map to accompany it. When you have completed your outline map, compare it with a map drawn by one other student.

Suppose now, we are back on the eastern shores of Lake Turkana 2½ million years ago. Standing by the shores we would be aware of crocodiles basking in the tropical heat on sand-spits pointing finger-like into the shallow water. A little more than five miles away to the east savanna-covered hills rise up from the lake basin, sliced here and there by forest-filled valleys. At one point the hills are breached by what is obviously a large river that has snaked its way down from the Ethiopian mountains. Where the river reaches the flood-plain of the lake it shatters into a delta of countless streams, some small, some large, but each fringed by a line of trees and bushes.

As we walk up one of the stream beds – dry now because there has been no rain for months – we might hear the rustle of a pig in search of roots and vegetation in the undergrowth. As the tree-cover thickens we catch a glimpse of a colobus monkey retreating through the tree tops. Lower down, mangobeys feed on the ripening figs. In the seclusion of the surrounding bushes small groups of impala and water-buck move cautiously. From the top of a tree we could see out into the open, where herds of gazelle graze.

After going about a mile up the stream we come across a scene that is strangely familiar. Before us is a group of eight creatures – definitely human-like, but definitely not truly human – some on the stream bed and some on its sandy bank.

(Adapted from R. Leakey and R. Lewin *People of the Lake*)

In academic writing it is more usual to describe a place using the bird's eye technique (as was done in the text in Task 4). Such a description may or may not be accompanied by a visual (a map, photograph, etc.). In novels and other writing which emphasizes the human aspect of a description, the pedestrian's view technique is often used (as in the text in Task 5).

Task 6

This text is not a geographical description, but a set of instructions on how to set up the equipment needed in order to produce an unusual photograph. First read the text and then try to draw a diagram showing how the equipment should be set up. Then check your diagram with the one on page 19.

Making a physiograph using a camera

To make a physiograph, place the camera on the floor with its lens pointing directly upwards and lying immediately below the torch which has been suspended from a hook in the ceiling on a piece of string. Two other strings are hung from hooks several inches to either side of the main string to which they are connected at a point, say, three-quarters of the way down so that they form a V. The strings and the torch should be so arranged that when the torch is given its first swing to set it in motion the movement of the light comes within the area of the negative in the camera. Turn the torch on, turn the room light off, set the torch swinging and open the shutter. Using a fast film, the aperture may be set at about F/11 but the correct stop will have to be discovered experimentally by tests. After several minutes' exposure the track made by the swinging light will have produced a delightful linear pattern on the negative and this can be enlarged in the ordinary way to make a white linear design on a black background.

(E. de Mare *Photography*)

Visuals are used by writers to achieve different goals. Sometimes they are used only to break up pages of text. However, in academic writing they usually have a more informative purpose. Sometimes this purpose is to duplicate information given in a text in order to help the reader visualize the relations more clearly. This can be seen in the 'Making a physiograph' text and the diagram on page 19. The visual clarifies the rather complicated spatial relations set out in the text. It is a good example of the old saying that 'a picture (map/plan/diagram) is worth a thousand words'.

Visuals are also used to supplement texts, i.e. to add further information to the text or to emphasize a different aspect of the information given in the text.

Task 7

Read the text and decide whether the map which accompanies it contains supplementary or duplicate information, and whether it is essential to an understanding of the text.

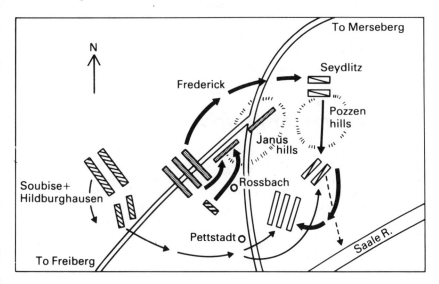

Rossbach *(The Seven Years War)*

Frederick II, the Great, faced his greatest peril in the summer of 1757. Prussia and its English ally had suffered successive defeats in the south (from Austria), west (from France), and east (from Russia). As the hostile ring tightened about him, the Prussian King rallied his forces and struck out to the west where the advance of 30,000 French and 11,000 Imperial troops of the Holy Roman Empire posed the greatest threat. In 12 days Frederick marched 170 miles to confront the invaders of Saxony at Rossbach, 26 miles southwest of Leipzig. The Prussians, reduced to 21,000 effective men by the forced march, camped northeast of the village.

On November 5 the allied commanders, the Prince de Soubise and the Prince of Saxe-Hildburghausen, resolved to crush Frederick with a large-scale turning movement against the Prussian left flank. Anticipating the manoeuver, Frederick deployed a small masking force to his front while his main body executed a leftward turning movement of its own behind a cover of hills. The ponderous allied columns, somewhat disorganised by a too-hasty march, suddenly received the full force of the Prussian blow on their right flank. Behind the fire of 18 heavy guns, Gen. Friedrich von Seydlitz' cavalry, followed by seven battalions of infantry, routed the enemy cavalry and then swooped down on the startled allied infantry. In 40 minutes the Prussian horsemen gunned and sabered the French and Imperials into wild flight. Most of the Prussian foot soldiers were still coming up when Soubise fled the field with 7,500 casualties, chiefly prisoners. The victors lost less than 600 men. Frederick's spectacular victory at Rossbach broke the advance from the west.

(D. Eggenberger *A Dictionary of Battles*)

Using grammar in writing

The most important information in a sentence very often appears at the beginning. This information may tell us what the sentence is about. For example, the sentence 'Zambia is a landlocked country' seems to be about Zambia. In this case 'Zambia' is also the subject of the sentence. However, in the sentence 'To the north lies Tanzania', 'To the north' is not the subject but is very important information as it locates the position of Tanzania in terms of some reference point which we already know.

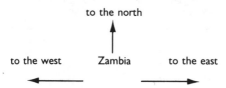

The organizing principle here is the points of the compass.

Task 8

Look at the following short texts and decide which is easier to understand.

i) I live in Edinburgh. The capital of Scotland is Edinburgh. A part of the British Isles is Scotland.
ii) I live in Edinburgh. It is the capital of Scotland. Scotland is part of the British Isles.

Text (ii) is easier to understand because the writer uses the beginning of each sentence to lead into the next, guiding us through the text in a logical way.

    I→Edinburgh→It (Edinburgh)→Scotland→Scotland→British Isles
The organizing principle here is from part to whole.

    In spatial descriptions you will find that locational expressions often appear at the beginning of sentences in the text (e.g. *Beside the river, Further south,* etc.).

Task 9

Read the spatial description which follows and underline the locational expressions that are used to guide the reader through the description.

Cairo: the modern city

The hub of the modern city of Cairo is the spacious Midan el-Tahrir (Liberation Square). Here all the city's main traffic arteries meet. – To the SW* of the square are the Ministry of Foreign Affairs and the Government Buildings, to the SE the American University and the National Assembly. To the NW of the square is the large range of buildings occupied by the Egyptian Museum, which has the world's largest and finest collection of Egyptian and Graeco-Roman antiquities. Just beyond the Egyptian Museum the Corniche el-Nil along the bank of the Nile is lined by large modern hotels and prestige buildings. In Shari Qasr el-Aini, which runs S from Midan el-Tahrir, is the Ethnological Museum, and in Shari el-Sheikh Rihan the Geological Museum. – To the NE of the Midan el-Tahrir are the main commercial and shopping districts of the modern city, which are entirely European in character. The goods sold in the shops here are marked with fixed prices, which cannot be reduced by bargaining like prices in the bazaars.

---

* SW = south west; NE = north east etc.

(*AA/Baedeker's Cairo*)

Descriptions of spatial locations are normally organized according to conventional ways of looking at scenes. The most common conventions are:

> general to particular
> whole to part
> large to small
> outside to inside
> top to bottom
> left to right

The main point here is to be consistent. If you choose a particular convention, use it throughout so as not to confuse the reader.

Task 10

a) Reread 'Cairo: the modern city' and state its organizing principle.
b) Draw a map of Cairo in as much detail as this text makes possible.

Appendix A

Task 11

a) Study the sketch map and then read the text which accompanies it. Notice how the writer has tried to organize both the whole text and each sentence, to guide your reading. Trace or copy out the map, then mark it with arrows (a red pen would be ideal) and number them to show the sequence in which the text describes it.

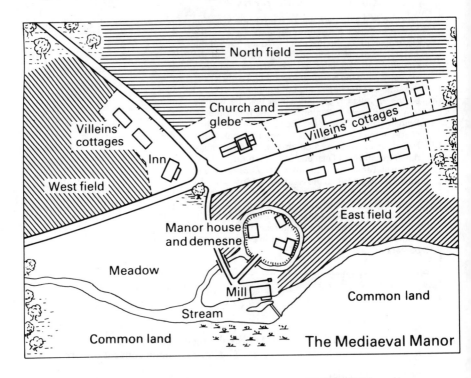

During the Middle Ages, the chief man of the village, or manor, was the lord of the manor. He owned his own piece of land on which he built his sturdy manor house. The lord's lands were known as the demesne and were usually walled, and separated from the rest of the village. The common lands of the manor were divided into three large fields: each field consisted of many long, narrow strips, and each villein (or villager) had a number of these strips, scattered about the field. Each year, wheat would be grown in one of the fields, barley or oats in another, and the third would be left uncultivated. A different field was left uncultivated each year to rest the soil.

The cottages of the villeins were built along the edges of

184

the fields beside the road, or track. These houses were simple buildings built of stone or wattle and daub (i.e. twigs and mud), and often had only one room. The church, with the priest's house and the glebe (the land belonging to the church) was in the middle of the village, frequently at a crossroads.

In addition to the fields of crops, the village had a hay meadow, usually near a stream. The hay was used for winter feed for the animals. The animals were kept on the common land on the outskirts of the village in good weather, and in bad weather they were brought into barns, or even into the villeins' houses.

(Adapted from J. Lockhart Whiteford *British History for the CSE Year*)

b) Reorganize the text, rewriting if necessary, so that it offers better guidance to the reader about the spatial relationships it describes.

Consolidation

A In some countries (the USA, for example) electric kettles are virtually unknown. Write a short text (imagine it is part of a letter to a penfriend in America) describing the main parts of an electric kettle and the way they fit together. The picture will help you.

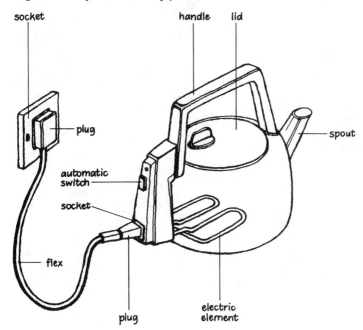

Appendix A

B   The outline map below shows the main car parks available to staff and
    students of Edinburgh University. Write a text, intended to be part of a letter
    to an overseas student planning to attend Edinburgh University, telling her
    she will need to apply for a parking permit, and suggesting the best car parks.
    Her classes will take place mainly in Adam Ferguson Building (marked AFB
    and shaded black on the map, and located to the south-east of George
    Square).

UNIVERSITY   OF   EDINBURGH

CAR PARKING AREAS

CENTRAL ZONES

Map Ref.	Area
A.	Appleton Tower
B.	Argyle Brewery, Cowgate
C.	Buccleuch Place Lane/ Meadow Lane East
D.	Forrest Hill
E.	George Square Lane
F.	Guthrie Street, Cowgate
G.	High School Yards
H.	Hume Tower Area/ Buccleuch Place West
I.	Maltings, Chambers St.
J.	Main Library
K.	Medical Buildings
L.	Meadow Lane West
M.	New College
N.	Old College
O.	Physical Education, Pleasance
P.	Physical Education (formerly EME garage)
Q.	Pfizer/Lister Institute
R.	Psychology, Pleasance
S.	Robertson's Close, Cowgate
T.	R(D)SVS., Summerhall
U.	South College Street
V.	St. Cecilia's Hall, Cowgate
W.	Students' Centre
X.	Usher Institute

PERIPHERAL ZONES

Y.	King's Buildings
Z.	Vet. Field Station

(Courtesy of University of Edinburgh)

186

C Imagine you are a dramatist. You have just written a drama, the major
portion of which is set in a living room just like the one pictured below.
Because dramatists never use pictures in their scripts, you have to write up
the stage scene. Organize the description from the audience's viewpoint (near
to far). Begin your description:

    We are looking at a living room . . .

Looking back

Now that you have completed this unit you should understand how texts are
organized according to a pedestrian's view and a bird's eye view. You should be
familiar with some expressions of location and understand how these are used
to guide a reader through a text; you should be able to use them in sentences and
text.

p. 12 Making a physiograph using a camera

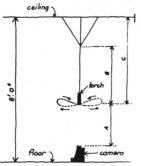

Making a physiograph: *A* is the distance between
camera lens and the light bulb of the swinging
torch; *B* is the distance between the light bulb
and the point in the string at which side strings
are fixed; *C* is the distance between light bulb
and ceiling. The relation between *B* and *C* sets
the pattern of the physiograph.

Extract 6

1 4 The Restaurant

14.1   Tune in

Look at the pictures and write the sentences into the speech bubbles.

> Would you like a drink while you're waiting?
>
> I'll have a mineral water thanks.
>
> I'll have a beer.

Have you ever been to a restaurant in Australia?
Think about the last restaurant you went to. Was it expensive?
Who did you go with?
Did you enjoy it?
Was it different from restaurants in
your own country?
In what ways?

14.2   Listen

Listen to the conversation and circle the words you hear.

1 a There were five of us, but we're up to nine.
  b There were nine of us but we're down to five.

2 a Would you like to go in the bar first?
  b Would you like a drink from the bar first?

3 a I'll have a drink of water.
  b I'll have a mineral water.

4 a Friends not here yet?
  b Are your friends here yet?

5 a We'll have a menu, too, please.
  b We'll have two menus please.

Listen again. How many questions do you hear? Circle the appropriate number.

   1   *3*   *5*   *7*   *9*

How many people are going to eat with the Barlows?
Are they going to eat inside or outside?
Are their friends early or late?
What do they have to drink?
What do they have to eat?

14.3 Read and discuss
Look at these advertisements.

RESTAURANT

The Seafood Inn

Licensed Cafe

We offer lunches or dinner in a casual relaxed atmosphere with indoor or outdoor seating. We have an interesting wine list and freshly prepared foods.

Phone us for bookings

HOURS
Tuesday to Friday
12.00-3.00 pm
6.30-11.30 pm

482 Spring Street Carlton
Ph. 306-2481

NORTH CHINA CHINESE RESTAURANT

We specialise in banquets and parties.
Authentic Chinese cuisine
Special lunchtime dishes

* Licenced or BYO *

SUNDAY DIM SUM LUNCH

Situated in Smithfield Shopping Centre

589 Walkley Road
Smithfield

Phone 361 9042

PEPPI'S ITALIAN RESTAURANT

Pasta just like Mama used to make

Fully licenced with Italian and Aust. wines or BYO

Open 7 Days for lunch and dinner

Car parking available

28 O'Connell Street
CITY

- Phone 2240186 -

PIZZA PALACE

PIZZA   DRAUGHT BEER   WINE
Fully licensed
Full take away service
Special children's menu
Everard Park, Glenelg, City

HAMBURGER JOE'S

Dine in or take away 7 days a week
friendly courteous waitress service
pleasant, informal air conditioned surroundings
Mon. Noon - 10 p.m.
Tues. Noon - 11 p.m.
Wed - Sat. Noon - Midnight
Sun Noon - 9 p.m.
14 Jetty Road, Glenelg
295 77 83

You are going to have these visitors over the next few weeks.
- 9 year old niece
- your parents
- your father-in-law
- an old school friend
- your younger brother

Which restaurant will you take them to? Why?
Which restaurant did the Barlows eat at? How do you know?

Where would you get these dishes?
Antipasto   *Baked schnapper*   Spaghetti napolitana   Oysters
Pizza Supreme   **Cheeseburger and chips**
Stir fried beef and snow peas   **Barbecued prawns**   *Spring rolls*
Sweet and sour pork   *Trout with butter sauce*   **Roast lamb**

Make a list of your favourite dishes. Which country/ countries are they from?

mawson House RESTAURANTS
Dine in the elegance of Mawson's or our informal Restaurant
The Rocks
Cocktail Lounge — Dancing Nightly
271 3955

14.4 Pronunciation

Listen to the tape:

	Unstressed	*Stressed*
	I'm	I **am**
	she's	she **is**
	they are	they **are**
	he was	he **was**
	we were	we **were**

Now read these sentences. Do you think the underlined words are stressed or unstressed? Put a circle around the stressed words.

A: It <u>was</u> a very nice restaurant we went to the other day.
B: <u>Were</u> the Barlows there?
A: Yes, they <u>were</u>. Peter <u>was</u> there too, but Anne <u>wasn't</u>.
B: <u>Is</u> it still open for lunch?
A: Yes, it <u>is</u>, although we <u>were</u> there for lunch of course.
       We might go again next week. <u>Are</u> you interested in coming?
B: Yes, I <u>am</u> as a matter of fact.

Now listen to the dialogue and make any corrections you like.
Compare your dialogue with a friend's.

14.5 Language focus

Read this conversation:
  Customer: *I'd like a bottle of mineral water, please.*
  Waiter: *Certainly, Sir. A big **one** or a small **one**?*
  Customer: *A small **one** will do.*
        One = bottle of mineral water.

What does 'one' refer to in these conversations?

A: I'd like some fish and a bowl of chips.
B: Sure. A large or a small one?
one: _____

A: I want a quiet table.
B: What about one by the window.
one: _____

A: There's no more wine in the bottle,
   Sir. Can I get you another one?
one: _____

A: Are there any Italian restaurants here?
B: Yes, there's a good one in Lee Street.
one: _____

Now look at this conversation
  Waiter: Would you like to go in the bar?
  Customer: No, I don't think **so**.
      so = go in the bar

*What does **so** refer to in these conversations?*

A: Is it nice outside?

B: Yes, I think so.
so: _____

A: Would you like a drink before
   ordering?
B: No, I don't think so.
so: _____

A: Do your friends know the way here?
B: I suppose so, yes.
so: _____

A: Would you like more garlic bread?
B: No, I don't think so.
so: _____

You are having a conversation, but don't hear every word.

Jane sat next to *noise*\\\\   You ask: Who did Jane sit next to?

noise\\\\ordered the fish.   You ask: Who ordered the fish?

What would you say here?

Alice called *noise*\\\\.	--->	_____	?
noise\\\\ brought the menu.	--->	_____	?
noise\\\\ wanted mineral water.	--->	_____	?
John ordered for *noise*\\\\.	--->	_____	?
They waited for *noise*\\\\.	--->	_____	?

14.6   Problem

Work in pairs and spot the mistakes. One student look at the order taken by the waiter. The other student look at the bill.

Order

Peppi's	
Date: *14 June* **Table:** *14* **Persons:** *6*	
2 X Antipasto	*14.00*
1 X Spaghetti Napolitana	*6.50*
1 X Calamari fritti	*8.00*
1 X Fettucini pesto	*6.50*
1 X Roast chicken	*12.50*
2 X Veal steak	*30.00*
2 X Grilled tuna	*32.00*
1 X Grilled liver	*14.00*
* Mixed salad (large)*	*8.50*
5 X coffee	*6.00*
	128.00

Bill

Peppi's	
Account No: 38642	
Waiter: 5	
Date: 14 June **Table:** 14 **Persons:** 5	
1 X Antipasto	7.00
2 X Spaghetti Napolitana	13.00
2 X Calamari fritti	16.00
1 X Fettucini pesto	6.50
2 X Roast chicken	25.50
1 X Veal steak	15.00
1 X Grilled tuna	16.00
2 X Grilled liver	28.00
Mixed salad (large)	9.50
4 X coffee	5.80
TOTAL:	142.30

14.7 Role play

Work with two other students. Each student take a different role.

Role A: You are the head waiter in a restaurant. You only have one table left, and must decide which of two groups should have it.

Role B: You are talking to the head waiter at a restaurant, and another customer. You have booked a table at the restaurant for family and friends to celebrate a new job you have just got. The other customer also wants a table. There is only one table left. You have to convince the waiter that you should have the table.

Role C: You are talking to the head waiter at a restaurant, and another customer. You do not have a booking, but want a table at the restaurant for family and friends to celebrate your daughter's birthday. She will be very disappointed if you do not get into the restaurant. The other customer also wants a table. There is only one table left. You have to convince the waiter that you should have the table.

14.8 Read, discuss and write

Read the following dialogue:

Waiter:	Right, then, who's ready to order?
Alice:	I will, if you like.
Waiter:	OK.
Alice:	What's the fish of the day?
Waiter:	Schnapper.
Alice:	I'll have that.
Waiter:	Grilled schnapper. Vegetables or salad with the fish Madam?
Alice:	Er, salad, please. Oh, and can I have some chips?
Waiter:	Certainly. And for you, Sir?
Tom:	I'll have the pepper steak.....

Make a list of all the dishes you like to eat. Work with two other students and take turns at ordering a meal.
Write a postcard to a friend about a restaurant meal you had recently.

Discuss your postcard with the teacher.

14.9   Learning focus

How do you like to learn English?
Put a number next to the following statements.

1	=	*not at all*
2	=	*a little*
3	=	*a lot*

1   I like to find my own mistakes when I am speaking.   ____

2   I like the teacher to correct my mistakes.   ____

3   I like people in the street/ shops etc. to correct me.   ____

4   I like the teacher to explain grammar to me.   ____

5   I like to learn grammar rules.   ____

6   I like to try and remember lots of new words.   ____

7   I like to write everything down.   ____

8   I like to find my own mistakes when I am writing.   ____

Compare your answers with a partner. Now discuss them with the teacher.

14.10   Out of class tasks

Look in the afternoon newspaper at the restaurant guide. Make a list of the restaurants you would like to visit. How many of these restaurants can you find in the Yellow Pages?

Call the restaurants and ask:

> Do you open on Sunday?
> Do you open for lunch?
> What time do you open during the week?

Look in your local paper. Find the restaurant guide.

> What's the cheapest restaurant?
> What's the most expensive?
> Where can you take your own wine?
> Which ones have entertainment?
> Which ones take credit cards?

Appendix B Approaches and methods — an overview

	Theory of language	Theory of learning	Objectives	Syllabus
Situational Language Teaching	Language is a set of structures; related to situations.	Memorisation and habit formation.	To teach a practical command of the four basic skills. Automatic, accurate control of basic sentence patterns. Oral before written mastery.	A list of structures and vocabulary graded according to grammatical difficulty.
Audiolingual	Language is a system of rule-governed structures hierarchically arranged.	Habit formation; skills are learned more effectively if oral precedes written; analogy not analysis.	Control of the structures of sound, form and order, mastery over symbols of the language; goal; native-speaker mastery.	Graded syllabus of phonology, morphology and syntax. Contrastive analysis.
Communicative	Language is a system for the expression of meaning; primary function-interaction and communication.	Activities involving real communication; carrying out meaningful tasks; and using language which is meaningful to the learner promote learning.	Objectives will reflect the needs of the learner; they will include functional skills as well as linguistic objectives.	Will include some/all of the following: structures functions, notions, themes, tasks. Ordering will be guided by learner needs.
Total Physical Response	Basically a structuralist, grammar based view of language.	L2 learning is the same as L1 learning; comprehension before production, is 'imprinted' through carrying out commands (right brain functioning) reduction of stress.	Teach oral proficiency to produce learners who can communicate uninhibitedly and intelligibly with native speakers.	Sentence-based syllabus with grammatical and lexical criteria being primary, but focus on meaning not form.
The Silent Way	Each language is composed of elements that give it a unique rhythm and spirit. Functional vocabulary and core structure are a key to the spirit of the language.	Processes of learning a second language are fundamentally different from L1 learning. L2 learning is an intellectual, cognitive process. Surrender to the music of the language, silent awareness then active trial.	Near-native fluency, correct pronunciation, basic practical knowledge of the grammar of the L2. Learner learn *how* to learn a language.	Basically structural lessons planned around grammatical items and related vocabulary. Items are introduced according to their grammatical complexity.
Community Language Learning	Language is more than a system for communication. It involves whole person, culture, educational, developmental communicative processes.	Learning involves the whole person. It is a social process of growth from child-like dependence to self-direction and independence.	No specific objectives. Near native mastery is the goal.	No set syllabus. Course progression is topic-based; learners provide the topics. Syllabus emerges from learners' intention and the teacher's reformulations.
The Natural Approach	The essence of language is meaning. Vocabulary not grammar is the heart of language.	There are two ways of L2 language development 'acquisition' – a natural subconscious process, and 'learning' – a conscious process. Learning cannot lead to acquisition.	Designed to give beginners and intermediate learners basic communicative skills. Four broad areas; basic personal communicative skills (oral/written); academic learning skills (oral/written).	Based on a selection of communicative activities and topics derived from learner needs.
Suggestopedia	Rather conventional, although memorisation of whole meaningful texts is recommended.	Learning occurs through suggestion, when learners are in a deeply relaxed state. Baroque music is used to induce this state.	To deliver advanced conversational competence quickly. Learners are required to master prodigious lists of vocabulary pairs, although the goal is understanding not memorisation.	Ten unit courses consisting of 1,200 word dialogues graded by vocabulary and grammar.

Activity types	Learner roles	Teacher roles	Roles of materials
Repetition, substitution drills; avoid translation and grammatical explanation; learners should never be allowed to make a mistake.	To listen and repeat, respond to questions and commands, learner has no control over content; later allowed to initiate statements and ask questions.	Acts as a model in presenting structures; orchestrates drill practice; corrects errors, tests progress.	Relies on textbook and visual aids; textbook contains tightly organised, structurally graded lessons.
Dialogues and drills, repetition and memorisation pattern practice.	Organisms that can be directed by skilled training techniques to produce correct responses.	Central and active teacher dominated method. Provides model, controls direction and pace.	Primarily teacher oriented. Tapes and visuals, language lab often used.
Engage learners in communication, involve processes such as information sharing, negotiation of meaning and interaction.	Learner as negotiator, interactor, giving as well as taking.	Facilitator of the communication process, participants tasks and texts, needs analyst, counsellor, process manager.	Primary role of promoting communicative language use; task-based materials; authentic.
Imperative drills to elicit physical actions.	Listener and performer, little influence over the content of learning.	Active and direct role 'the director of a stage play' with students as actors.	No basic text; materials and media have an important role later. Initially voice, action and gestures are sufficient.
Learner responses to commands, questions and visual cues. Activities encourage and shape oral responses without grammatical explanation or modelling by teacher.	Learning is a process of personal growth. Learners are responsible for their own learning and must develop independence autonomy and responsibility.	Teachers must a) teach b) test c) get out of the way. Remain impassive. Resist temptation to model, remodel, assist, direct exhort.	Unique materials: coloured rods, colour-coded pronunciation and vocabulary charts.
Combination of innovative and conventional. Translation, group work, recording, transcription, reflection and observation, listening, free conversation.	Learners are members of a community. Learning is not viewed as an individual accomplishment, but something that is achieved collaboratively.	Counselling/parental analogy. Teacher provides a safe environment in which students can learn and grow.	No textbook, which would inhibit growth. Materials are developed as course progresses.
Activities allowing comprehensible input, about things in the here-and-now. Focus on meaning not form.	Should not try and learn language in the usual sense, but should try and lose themselves in activities involving meaningful communication.	The teacher is the primary source of comprehensible input. Must create positive low-anxiety climate. Must choose and orchestrate a rich mixture of classroom activities.	Materials come from realia rather then textbooks. Primary aim is to promote comprehension and communication.
Initiatives, question and answer, role play, listening exercises under deep relaxation.	Must maintain a passive state and allow the materials to work on them (rather than vice versa).	To create situations in which the learner is most suggestible and present material in a way most likely to encourage positive reception and retention. Must exude authority and confidence.	Consists of texts, tapes, classroom fixtures and music. Texts should have force, literary quality and interesting characters.

Appendix C   Graded activities for the four macroskills

In this appendix you will find sets of activities for the four macroskills which are graded into seven levels of difficulty. These may be useful in the development of your own learning tasks.

Listening

Level 1

- distinguish between English and other languages
- listen to short aural texts and indicate (e.g. by putting up hand) when core vocabulary items are heard
- identify the number and gender of interlocutors
- comprehend and carry out the following instructions: point to, touch, stand up, sit down, go to ____, pick up, put down
- comprehend requests for personal details (name, age, address)
- comprehend requests for the identification of people and things
- listen to simple descriptions of common objects (e.g. those found in the classroom and/or immediate environment) and identify these non-verbally (e.g. by drawing a picture)
- identify letters of the alphabet and numbers to fifty including ten/teen contrasts
- listen to and identify the time

Level 2

- identify core vocabulary items when encountered in a variety of aural texts
- comprehend and carry out a sequence of two to three instructions
- comprehend requests for details about family and friends
- comprehend requests for identification of people and things
- listen to simple descriptions of actions and scenes and identify these non-verbally (e.g. by finding a picture, numbering pictures in the order in which they are described)
- given contextual/pictorial support, can comprehend simple descriptions
- identify ordinal numbers 1–10
- listen to and identify days of the week, months and dates

Level 3

- identify core vocabulary items when encountered in a variety of aural texts
- comprehend and carry out a sequence of four to five instructions
- develop factual discrimination skills by listening to a passage and identifying true/false statements relating to the passage
- comprehend requests for factual information relating to topic areas
- listen to a short aural text and transform the information by presenting it in a different form (e.g. by completing a table or diagram)

Level 4

- identify core vocabulary items when encountered in a variety of aural texts
- develop inferencing skills by listening to a passage and identifying true/false inferences relating to the passage
- comprehend requests for factual and attitudinal information relating to topic areas
- listen to a short aural text and transform the information by presenting it in a different form (e.g. by completing a table or diagram)
- comprehend and carry out a linked set of instructions
- grasp the gist of a short narrative
- identify emotional state of speaker from tone and intonation

Level 5

- identify core vocabulary items when encountered in a variety of aural texts
- develop inferencing skills by listening to a passage and identifying true/false inferences relating to the passage
- comprehend requests for factual and attitudinal information relating to topic areas
- listen to a short aural text and transform the information by presenting it in a different form (e.g. by completing a table or diagram)

Level 6

- identify core vocabulary items when encountered in a variety of aural texts
- develop inferencing skills by listening to a passage and suggesting an appropriate conclusion
- comprehend requests for factual and attitudinal information relating to topic areas
- listen to a short aural text and transform the information by presenting it in a different form (e.g. by completing a table or diagram)
- comprehend a short narrative when events are reported out of sequence

Level 7

- extract detailed information from a text
- grasp the gist of an extended text

Appendix C

- follow an extended set of instructions
- differentiate between fact and opinion
- identify the genre and register of a text
- recognise differences in intonation
- identify relationships between participants in aural interactions
- identify the emotional tone of an utterance
- comprehend the details of short conversations on unfamiliar topics

Speaking and oral interaction

Level 1

- name common objects
- give personal details such as name, age and address
- memorise and recite songs and rhymes in chorus
- take part in short, contextualised dialogues
- give simple (single clause) descriptions of common objects
- request goods and objects
- make statements of ability about self and others

Level 2

- describe family and friends (e.g. refer to age, relationship, size, weight, hair and eye colouring)
- recite songs and rhymes in chorus and individually
- ask and make statements about the likes of self and others
- spell out words from core vocabulary list, and say words when they are spelled out
- answer questions/give details of simple descriptions following an aural presentation
- request details about the family and friends of others using cue words
- make short (one to two sentence) statements on familiar topics using cue words
- talk about regularly occurring activities
- compute quantities and money in English
- tell the time in hours and half hours

Level 3

- answer questions/give details following an aural presentation
- make short (three to four sentence) statements on familiar topics
- following a model, make a series of linked statements about a picture, map, chart or diagram
- work in pairs/small groups to share information and solve a problem
- tell the time using fractions of an hour
- describe a short sequence of past events using sentence cues
- make complete statements from sentence cues given appropriate contextual support

198

— make comparisons between physical objects and entities
— use conversational formulae for greeting and leavetaking

Level 4

— answer questions, give details of descriptions following an aural presentation
— describe a picture related to a specific topic area
— narrate a linked sequence of past events shown in a picture sequence or cartoon strip
— work in groups to solve problems which require making inferences and establishing causality
— give opinions about specified issues and topics
— use conversational and discourse strategies e.g. to change subject, provide additional information, invite another person to speak
— give a sequence of directions
— make requests and offers
— talk about future events

Level 5

— give a short summary of the main points of an aural presentation
— give a detailed description of a picture relating to a familiar scene
— describe a simple process
— describe a linked sequence of actions
— work in groups to solve problems requiring the integration of information from a variety of aural and written sources
— give opinions about specified issues and topics
— use conversational and discourse strategies of holding the floor, disagreeing, qualifying what has been said

Level 6

— give a detailed summary of the main points and supporting details of an aural presentation
— give a prepared oral presentation on a familiar topic
— give a short aural presentation relating to information presented non-textually (e.g. as a chart, map, diagram or graph)
— describe complex processes with the aid of a diagram
— describe a sequence of events in a variety of tenses
— work in groups to solve problems requiring the resolution of conflicting information
— comprehend and convey messages by telephone
— qualify one's opinion through the use of modality
— use appropriate non-verbal behaviour

Level 7

— give an unprepared oral presentation on a familiar topic
— use a range of conversational styles from formal to informal

Appendix C

- work in groups to solve problems involving hypothesising and relating to abstract topics
- initiate and respond to questions of abstract topics
- use a range of conversational and discourse strategies

Reading

Level 1

- sight read all the words in the core vocabulary list when encountered in context
- read the names of class members
- read the written equivalent of numbers 1–60
- read short contextualised lists e.g. shopping lists
- decode regular sound symbol correspondences
- read single sentence descriptions of familiar objects

Level 2

- sight read all the words in the core vocabulary list when encountered in and out of context
- read short (two to three sentence) passages on familiar topics and answer yes/no and true/false questions relating to factual details
- read written equivalent of numbers 1–100
- read prices and quantities
- decode consonant clusters
- read sentences which have been mastered orally

Level 3

- read short (three to five sentence) passages and answer yes/no and wh-questions relating to factual detail
- read short (three to five sentence) passages and identify correct inferential statements relating to the passage
- read and interpret information presented as a chart or timetable
- dictate a story to the teacher and then read it

Level 4

- read two to three paragraph story on familiar topic and select main idea from a list of alternatives
- arrange scrambled sentences and paragraphs into the correct order
- develop dictionary skills (alphabetical order and indexes)
- follow linked series of written instructions
- read a short passage and predict what will happen next by selecting from a list of alternatives
- scan a three to five paragraph text for given key words
- identify the antecedents of anaphoric reference items

Level 5

- read three to five paragraph text and state the main idea
- scan a five to ten paragraph text for given key words
- identify logical relationships marked by conjunctions in three to five paragraph texts on familiar topics
- scan large texts (e.g. dictionary; telephone book) for specific information
- read a short story on a familiar topic and give a short oral summary

Level 6

- read a five to ten paragraph text on a familiar topic and state the main ideas
- read a five to ten paragraph text and present the key information in a non-textual form (e.g. by completing a table or graph)
- identify logical relationships marked by conjunctions in five to ten paragraph texts on unfamiliar topics
- follow a narrative or description when the ideas and events are presented in sequence
- differentiate between fact and opinion

Level 7

- read a five to ten paragraph text on an unfamiliar topic and state the main ideas and supporting details
- identify unmarked logical relationships in five to ten paragraph texts on unfamiliar topics
- follow a narrative or description when the ideas and events are presented out of sequence
- identify instances of bias in a written text
- understand underlying purpose/function of text
- differentiate between relevant and irrelevant information

Writing

Level 1

- write letters of the alphabet in upper and lower case
- write numbers 1–60
- write own name and names of other students and family members
- copy legibly words in core vocabulary list
- copy legibly short messages and lists (e.g. shopping lists)
- complete short contextualised description of person or object

Level 2

- write figures 1–100
- use capital letters and periods appropriately
- write legibly and accurately words in core vocabulary list
- write short, familiar sentences when dictated

Level 3

— complete short contextualised description of person or object
— write short, familiar sentences when dictated
— write words and clauses in legible cursive script
— rewrite scrambled sentences as coherent paragraph

Level 4

— write short, personal note on familiar topic to a friend (e.g. on post card)
— write short (one sentence) answer to comprehension questions
— take short (single paragraph) dictation from familiar text
— create paragraph from individual sentences using cohesion to link sentences

Level 5

— write a short description of a familiar object or scene
— write short (two to three sentence) answers to comprehension questions
— write single paragraph conclusion to a narrative
— take short (single paragraph) dictation from an unfamiliar text
— develop fluency through free writing activities

Level 6

— write summary in point form/précis of a short aural or written text
— produce a text from data provided in non-text form (e.g. as table, graph, or chart)
— write a single paragraph conclusion to a passage presenting an argument
— take a three to five paragraph dictation from a familiar text

Level 7

— use appropriate punctuation conventions
— write a short essay using paragraphs to indicate main information units
— write quickly without pausing, erasing or correcting as part of the process of drafting or composing
— use pre-writing strategies as a preparation for writing
— use revision strategies to polish one's initial efforts

This is adapted from an unpublished seven-level syllabus developed by the author for an ESL curriculum.

Cumulative bibliography

Abbs, B., C. Candlin, C. Edelhoff, T. Moston, and M. Sexton. 1978. *Challenges: Students' Book*. London: Longman.

Alexander, L. 1967. *Practice and Progress Part 2*. London: Longman.

Anderson, A., and T. Lynch. 1988. *Listening*. Oxford: Oxford University Press.

Asher, J. 1977. *Learning Another Language Through Actions: The Complete Teacher's Guide Book*. Los Gatos Calif.: Sky Oaks Productions.

Bell, J., and B. Burnaby. 1984. *A Handbook for ESL Literacy*. Toronto: OISE.

Bransford, J., and M. Johnson. 1972. Contextual prerequisites for understanding: some investigations of comprehension and recall. *Journal of Verbal Learning and Verbal Recall*, 11, 717–26.

Breen, M. 1984. Processes in syllabus design. In C. Brumfit (Ed.) *General English Syllabus Design*. Oxford: Pergamon Press.

Breen, M. 1987. Learner contributions to task design. In Candlin and Murphy.

Breen, M., and C. Candlin. 1980. The essentials of a communicative curriculum in language teaching. *Applied Linguistics*, 1 (2), 89–112.

Brindley, G. 1987. Factors affecting task difficulty. In Nunan 1987b.

Brosnan, D., K. Brown, and S. Hood. 1984. *Reading in Context*. Adelaide: National Curriculum Resource Centre.

Brown, G., and G. Yule. 1983. *Teaching the Spoken Language*. Cambridge: Cambridge University Press.

Brumfit, C. 1984. *Communicative Methodology in Language Teaching*. Cambridge: Cambridge University Press.

Brundage, D. H., and MacKeracher, D. 1980. *Adult Learning Principles and their Application to Program Planning*. Ontario: Ontario Institute for Studies in Education.

Bygate, M. 1987. *Speaking*. Oxford: Oxford University Press.

Candlin, C. 1987. Toward task-based learning. In Candlin and Murphy.

Candlin, C., and C. Edelhoff. 1982. *Challenges: Teacher's Book*. London: Longman.

Candlin, C., and D. Murphy (Eds.). 1987. *Language Learning Tasks*. Englewood Cliffs NJ: Prentice-Hall.

Candlin, C., and D. Nunan. 1987. *Revised Syllabus Specifications for the Omani School English Language Curriculum*. Muscat: Ministry of Education and Youth.

Carnicelli, T. 1980. The writing conference: a one-to-one conversation. In T. Donovan and B. McClelland (Eds.) *Eight Approaches to Teaching Conversation*. Urbana Ill.: National Council of Teachers of English.

Carrell, P., J. Devine, and D. Eskey (Eds.). 1988. *Interactive Approaches to Second Language Reading*. Cambridge: Cambridge University Press.

Bibliography

Chaudron, C. 1988. *Second Language Classrooms: Research on Teaching and Learning*. Cambridge: Cambridge University Press.

Clark, J. 1987. *Curriculum Renewal in School Foreign Language Learning*. Oxford: Oxford University Press.

Clarke, M., and S. Silberstein. 1977. Toward a realization of psycholinguistic principles in the ESL reading class. *Language Learning*, 27 (1), 48–65.

Clemens, J., and J. Crawford. 1986. *Lifelines*. Adelaide: National Curriculum Resource Centre.

Coe, N., R. Rycroft, and P. Ernest. 1983. *Writing Skills: A Problem-Solving Approach*. Cambridge: Cambridge University Press.

Comeau, R. 1987. Interactive oral grammar exercises. In Rivers.

Curran, C. 1976. *Counselling–Learning in Second Language*. Apple River Ill.: Apple River Press.

Dickinson, L. 1987. *Self-Instruction in Language Learning*. Cambridge: Cambridge University Press.

Di Pietro, R. 1987. *Strategic interaction*. Cambridge: Cambridge University Press.

Doff, A., C. Jones, and K. Mitchell. 1983. *Meaning into Words: Intermediate*. Cambridge: Cambridge University Press.

Doughty, C., and T. Pica. 1986. 'Information gap' tasks: Do they facilitate second language acquisition? *TESOL Quarterly*, 20 (2), 305–25.

Dubin, F., and E. Olshtain. 1986. *Course Design: Developing Programs and Materials for Language Learning*. Cambridge: Cambridge University Press.

Duff, P. 1986. Another look at interlanguage talk: Taking tasks to task. In R. Day (Ed.) *Talking to Learn*. Rowley Mass.: Newbury House.

Evans, R. 1986. *Learning English Through Content Areas: The Topic Approach to ESL*. Melbourne: Ministry of Education.

Forrester, H., L. Palmer, and P. Spinks. 1986. *It's Over to You*. Adelaide: Department of Technical and Further Education.

Goodman, K. 1971. Psycholinguistic universals in the reading process. In P. Pimsleur and T. Quinn (Eds.) *The Psychology of Second Language Learning*. Cambridge: Cambridge University Press.

Grellet, F. 1981. *Developing Reading Skills*. Cambridge: Cambridge University Press.

Hamp-Lyons, L., and B. Heasley. 1987. *Study Writing*. Cambridge: Cambridge University Press.

Hover, D. 1986a. *Think Twice: Teacher's Book*. Cambridge: Cambridge University Press.

Hover, D. 1986b. *Think Twice: Students' Book*. Cambridge: Cambridge University Press.

Jones, L. 1984. *Ideas*. Cambridge: Cambridge University Press.

Jones, L. 1985. *Use of English*. Cambridge: Cambridge University Press.

Jones, M., and R. Moar. 1985. *Listen to Australia*. Adelaide: National Curriculum Resource Centre.

Knowles, M. 1983. *The Adult Learner: A Neglected Species*. Houston: Gulf Publishing Company.

Krashen, S., and T. Terrell. 1983. *The Natural Approach*. Oxford: Pergamon Press.

Littlewood, W. 1981. *Communicative Language Teaching – An Introduction.* Cambridge: Cambridge University Press.

Long, M. 1985. A role for instruction in second language acquisition. In K. Hyltenstam and M. Pienemann (Eds.). 1985. *Modelling and Assessing Second Language Acquisition.* Clevedon Avon.: Multilingual Matters.

Long, M., L. Adams, and F. Castanos. 1976. Doing things with words: Verbal interaction in lockstep and small group classroom situations. In R. Crymes and J. Fanselow (Eds.) *On TESOL '76.* Washington DC: TESOL.

Maley, A., and S. Moulding. 1981. *Learning to Listen.* Cambridge: Cambridge University Press.

McArthur, T. 1984. *The Written Word: A Course in Controlled Composition.* Oxford: Oxford University Press.

Montgomery, C., and M. Eisenstein. 1982. Real reality revisited: An experimental communicative course in ESL. *TESOL Quarterly,* 19, 2.

Morris, A., and N. Stewart-Dore. 1984. *Learning to Learn from Text: Effective Reading in the Content Areas.* Sydney: Addison-Wesley.

Nunan, D. 1982. *What Do You Think?* Adelaide: Language Press.

Nunan, D. 1984. Discourse processing by first language, second phase and second language learners. Unpublished doctoral dissertation. The Flinders University of South Australia.

Nunan, D. 1985a. *Language Teaching Course Design: Trends and Issues.* Adelaide: National Curriculum Resource Centre.

Nunan, D. 1985b. Content familiarity and the perception of textual relationships in second language reading. *RELC Journal,* 16 (1), 43–51.

Nunan, D. 1987a. *The Teacher as Curriculum Developer.* Adelaide: National Curriculum Resource Centre.

Nunan, D. 1987b. *Guidelines for the Development of Curriculum Resources.* Adelaide: National Curriculum Resource Centre.

Nunan, D. 1988a. *The Learner-Centred Curriculum.* Cambridge: Cambridge University Press.

Nunan, D. 1988b. *Syllabus Design.* Oxford: Oxford University Press.

Nunan, D. 1989. *Syllabus Specifications for the Omani School English Language Curriculum.* Sultanate of Oman: Ministry of Education and Youth.

Nunan, D., and J. Lockwood. 1988. *The Australian English Course: Level 1. Draft Pilot Edition.* Cambridge: Cambridge University Press.

Ostrander, S., and L. Schroeder. 1981. *Superlearning.* London: Sphere Books.

Parker, K., and C. Chaudron. 1987. The effects of linguistic simplification and elaborative modifictions on L2 comprehension. Manuscript.

Pattison, P. 1987. *Developing Communication Skills.* Cambridge: Cambridge University Press.

Pearson, P. D., and D. D. Johnson. 1972. *Teaching Reading Comprehension.* New York: Holt, Rinehart and Winston.

Perl, S. 1980. A look at basic writers in the process of composing. In L. Kasden and D. Hoeber (Eds.) *Basic Writing.* Urbana Ill.: National Council of Teachers of English.

Pica, T., and C. Doughty. 1985. The role of groupwork in classroom second language acquisition. *Studies in Second Language Acquisition,* 7, 233–48.

Pienemann, M., and M. Johnston. 1987. Factors influencing the development of language proficiency. In D. Nunan (Ed.) *Applying Second Language Acquisition Research.* Adelaide: National Curriculum Resource Centre.

Porter, D., and J. Roberts. 1981. Authentic listening activities. *English Language Teaching Journal.* 36 (1), 37–47.

Prabhu, N. 1987. *Second Language Pedagogy: A Perspective.* Oxford: Oxford University Press.

Prowse, P., J. Garton-Sprenger, and T. C. Jupp. 1981. *Exchanges: Students' Book.* London: Heinemann.

Ramani, E. 1987. Theorizing from the classroom. *English Language Teaching Journal,* 41 (1), 3–11.

Richards, J. 1987a. Designing instructional materials for teaching listening comprehension. Unpublished manuscript.

Richards, J. 1987b. Beyond methods: alternative approaches to intructional design in language teaching. *Prospect,* 3(1), 11–30.

Richards, J., and T. Rodgers. 1986. *Approaches and Methods in Language Teaching.* Cambridge: Cambridge University Press.

Richards, J., J. Platt, and H. Weber. 1986. *Longman Dictionary of Applied Linguistics.* London: Longman.

Rivers, W. (Ed.). 1987. *Interactive Language Teaching.* Cambridge: Cambridge University Press.

Rivers, W., and M. Temperley. 1978. *A Practical Guide to the Teaching of English as a Second or Foreign Langue.* New York: Oxford University Press.

Robinson, C. 1977. *Advanced Use of English: A Coursebook.* London: Hamish Hamilton.

Rubin, J., and I. Thompson. 1982. *The Good Language Learner.* Boston Mass.: Heinle and Heinle.

Rutherford, W. 1987. *Second Language Grammar: Learning and Teaching.* London: Longman.

Scarcella, R. 1978. Socio-drama for social interaction. *TESOL Quarterly,* 12, 41–6.

Seliger, H., and M. Long. 1983. *Classroom-Oriented Research.* Rowley Mass.: Newbury House.

Shavelson, R., and P. Stern. 1981. Research on teachers' pedagogical thoughts, judgements, decisions and behaviour. *Review of Educational Research,* 51 (4), 455–98.

Slade, D., and L. Norris. 1986. *Teaching Casual Conversation.* Adelaide: National Curriculum Resource Centre.

Smith, F. 1978. *Reading.* Cambridge: Cambridge University Press.

Sommers, N. 1980. Revision strategies of student writers and experienced adult writers. *College Composition and Communication,* 31, 4.

Stanovich, K. 1980. Toward an interactive-compensatory model of individual differences in the development of reading fluency. *Reading Research Quarterly,* 16, 32–71.

Stenhouse, L. 1975. *An Introduction to Curriculum Research and Development.* London: Heinemann.

Strevens, P. 1987. Interaction outside the classroom: using the community. In Rivers.

Swaffar, J., K. Arens, and M. Morgan. 1982. Teacher classroom practices: redefining methods as task hierarchy. *Modern Language Journal*, 66, 1.

Tyler, R. 1949. *Basic Principles of Curriculum and Instruction.* New York: Harcourt Brace.

Varonis, E., and S. Gass. 1983. Target language input from non-native speakers. Paper presented at the Seventeenth Annual TESOL Convention, Toronto.

Wells, G. 1981. *Learning through Interaction.* Cambridge: Cambridge University Press.

White, R. 1981. Approaches to writing. *Guidelines*, 6, 1–11.

Whitney, N. 1983. *Checkpoint English 1.* Oxford: Oxford University Press.

Widdowson, H. 1978. *Teaching Language as Communication.* Oxford: Oxford University Press.

Widdowson, H. 1987. Aspects of syllabus design. In M. Tickoo (Ed.) *Language Syllabuses: State of the Art.* Singapore: RELC.

Wilkins, D. 1976. *Notional Syllabuses.* Oxford: Oxford University Press.

Willing, K. 1988. *Learning Styles in Adult Migrant Education.* Adelaide: National Curriculum Resource Centre.

Wright, T. 1987a. Instructional task and discoursal outcome in the L2 classroom. In Candlin and Murphy.

Wright, T. 1987b. *Roles of Teachers and Learners.* Oxford: Oxford University Press.

Zamel, V. 1982. Writing: the process of discovering meaning. *TESOL Quarterly*, 16 (2), 495–9.

Zuern, G. 1985. *Images 1.* Reading Ma.: Addison-Wesley.

Index

Subject index

accuracy versus fluency 63–4
action research 145
activity *see also* information gap,
  problem solving, role play
  evaluation 137
  grading and difficulty 104–8
  types 64–76
audiolingual method 80, 133, 144,
  194–5
Australian English Course, Pilot Edition
  188–93
Australian Language Levels (ALL)
  Project 49–50
authenticity 54–8, 59–60, 138

Bangalore Project 42–4, 66–7, 112

Challenges 119–22, 131, 151–63
classroom-centred research 44, 122
classroom interaction 87–90, 128–30
communicative language teaching
  12–14, 19, 86–90, 194–5
community-based learning 93
Community Language Learning 80,
  133, 144, 194–5
content area instruction 58, 125–7
curriculum development 14–19
  and classroom practice, 144–5

English for Specific Purposes 50–1

General Purpose English 50–1
genre *see* text types
goals 41, 48–52, 135
grammar 13, 38, 74, 82–3, 97–8,
  123

humanistic education 94, 133

independent learning 83–4
information gap 64–6, 122–4
input 53–9, 97–101, 136
inservice *see* teacher development
INSET *see* teacher development
interaction *see* classroom
  interaction

learner
  assessment 137
  -centred philosophy, 19–20, 94
  groups 91–2
  roles *see* roles – learner
learning
  as rehearsal 41
  -how-to-learn 80–4
  strategies 80–4
Learning to Listen 7–9
Lifelines 56
Listen to Australia 104–8
listening
  activities 64–9
  conversational versus academic 24–5
  interactional and transactional 26
  nature of 23–6
  top-down and bottom-up processing
  26

Meaning into Words Intermediate 52
methodology 1, 15
methods 2, 79–80, 143–4, 194–5

Natural Approach 80, 144, 194–5
needs analysis 40

Author index